GW00729101

THE NIGHT
CAME

The Night the Rain Came In continues the adventures
of Louisa, Japhet and Rose Brown, the family first
encountered in *The Day the Ceiling Fell Down*.
Originally published in 1963, this story has all the
elements of a Jenifer Wayne classic: the everyday
humour and chaos of family life, unexpected develop-
ments in the plot, vivid and realistic dialogue and some
perfectly observed and sketched minor characters,
such as the lorry-driving man from Pinks' Ladders, and
the wool-shop lady from the fire station. This last ability,
likened by one critic to the work of Stella Gibbons, is
perhaps in part a legacy of Jenifer Wayne's time as a
writer and producer for the Features Department of
BBC Radio, where she worked from 1941–1948.

Born in London in 1917, and educated at Somerville
College, Oxford, Jenifer Wayne has written many other
novels and stories for children, among them six stories
about a little boy called Sprout. In 1948 Jenifer Wayne
married the journalist C. H. Rolph. She died in 1982.

St. HELEN'S SCHOOL
LIBRARY

St Helen's School Northwood

T14926

THE NIGHT THE RAIN CAME IN

Jenifer Wayne

THE BODLEY HEAD
LONDON

British Library Cataloguing
in Publication Data
Wayne, Jenifer
The night the rain came in.—(Bodley bookshelf)
I. Title
823'.914[J]   PZ7
ISBN 0-370-30798-4

Copyright © Jenifer Wayne 1963
Printed and bound in Finland for
The Bodley Head Ltd
30 Bedford Square, London WC1B 3RP
by Werner Söderström Oy

First published by William Heinemann Ltd 1963
This edition first published by The Bodley Head Ltd 1986

Chapter One

H<small>E CAME</small> at dusk on September evenings, with a Tilley lamp. This is an oil lamp which gives a faint hiss and a golden light.

'And you can warm your hands by it, too,' he said.

He always wore a cap, and tucked his trousers into wellington boots; and under each arm he had a white knobbly paper bag. They didn't know his name; he was just the mushroom man.

He would put the lamp down under the back porch while he waited for the money.

'Three shillings a pound is cheap, isn't it?' Louisa asked her mother, who said Yes, and poked a knife into Rose's tin money-box. The mushroom man never had any change, nor did Louisa's mother; so there was often this poking of money-boxes, or somebody might try the old honey-jar at the bottom of the boiler-cupboard, or of course there was always that vase on the kitchen mantelpiece, full of press-studs and pieces of chocolate, rubber bands, school badges that ought to have been sewn on – and perhaps the odd sixpence.

The vase will tell you that this was not a tidy family. Louisa, who was fourteen, was very tidy indeed in her school-books, but her bedroom was a clutter of clothes underfoot and cardboard boxes with things sticking out all round.

Japhet was ten, and for some reason of his own kept a tea-pot in his bedroom. He never used it; it was cracked, and he didn't drink tea anyway. But it stood on a blue shelf between two sheeps' skulls; on the same shelf was a pile of old comics, some dusty electric-train buffers, and a very stiff small jacket that Japhet had once made for a limp velvet bear. He was still fond of this bear, though he wouldn't have said so to anyone outside the family. But the jacket, made of a tablecloth corner, was much too stiff to fit. The blue shelf had been meant for books; but these lay about the rest of the room, with odd slippers and sometimes a banana skin.

Rose, the youngest – eight – was not really yet able to look after her bedroom or anything else. She was vague. She did write herself notes from time to time, such as 'Fridays are best'; or 'One day when I was young I had a short cut and it did not look nice.' Their mother kept these notes when she found them, but the others thought them rather pointless. And they made the room more untidy than ever.

But we left the mushroom man at the back door. And this time there was no change – only sixpence in

2

Rose's money-box. 'And that's her tooth sixpence,' remarked Louisa. 'She'll make an awful fuss.'

'I'll put it back tomorrow,' said their mother, but it was no use, as she couldn't find the half-crown she thought was at the bottom of her bursting handbag.

So Louisa went to the back door to offer a ten-shilling note, or to pay next time.

'Next time'll have to do,' said the mushroom man rather sourly. He wouldn't touch the note.

'Mind, I don't know as there'll *be* a next time,' he added. 'Pretty well finished now. Been a bad do, this year.'

'Why, haven't they been growing well?' Louisa asked.

'Rotten. The best's what *you've* had.' He sounded annoyed at that, too. 'I shall probably pack it in. Not worth it.'

He picked up the lamp, which lit the underneath of the eaves and the thin set of his face. Outside the hissing gold the garden was nearly dark, with a white ground-mist creeping across from the field.

'Turning chilly, isn't it? They said on the radio sixty-five shopping days till Christmas.' Louisa always did her best to make conversation; she smiled amicably.

'Hm. Christmas,' said the man, not smiling back. 'Bad enough now, without thinking about Christmas. 'Night.'

And he rode off on his high old bicycle, with the

3

lamp swinging on the handle-bar.

'I don't like him much,' Louisa said to her mother.

'Oh well, I think he has a rather hard life.'

'Why?' asked Japhet. He was pouring himself a huge glass of milk; his mother sighed and wondered if she ought to stop him: he was getting such a bulky boy. 'Why?' He wiped his mouth with his hand, and his hand on his jeans.

'Well . . .' And their mother told them the little she knew about the mushroom man. Just that his wife had died some years ago, and he worked on Mertons' farm, and had one boy who had passed into the Grammar School and wanted to go to Cambridge.

'So the mushrooms are a side-line,' added their mother, 'to try and make ends meet, I suppose.'

'What ends?' Rose always seemed to come in half-way through a conversation, so that everything had to be explained again.

'Not that it makes much difference if she's there all the time,' Louisa would comment.

At that moment Rose did get one point, which was that a plasticine head had fallen on its face and would never be the same again. Their mother tried thumbing in new cheekbones and saying that it would just be a *different* face; Japhet rudely told Rose to belt up; Louisa said, 'Howling won't help,' and sat down to do her algebra between a plate of old bread-and-butter and a kilner jar of Japhet's water-beetles.

'I know that boy,' said Japhet; 'he's the one with spectacles who goes on the bus.'

'What boy? Who? Where?' Rose gazed round at them with a wet face and a turned-down mouth.

'Your slide's coming out,' said Louisa placidly.

'Oh shuddup!' Rose yelled. '*What* boy? That's all I want to know!'

When the scene had died down, and Rose was sitting in the bath eating a piece of cheese, Japhet came back to Louisa in the kitchen. His blue eyes were opened as wide as possible – but don't get this wrong; they were rather small eyes, and his pink face was round.

'I say, I've got an idea!'

'I thought it was "Scarface" tonight,' said Louisa, as if she were not particularly pleased to see him. She was on geography now, and had just been taking her mapping-pen out of its bit of cotton wool.

'It is,' said Japhet, 'but End of Part One. Listen: why don't *we* grow mushrooms?'

'Whatever for?' Louisa began to trace Pakistan, regardless.

'Then we could give them to the mushroom man and he could sell them and have the money!'

'Don't be silly, he wouldn't do that.'

'Well, charge him just a bit, then, and he can sell them for more.'

St. HELEN'S SCHOOL
LIBRARY

'Why?' asked Louisa, unmoved.

'To help him, of course,' said Japhet. Louisa glanced up; she may have been a comfortable-looking girl, but her glances could make people quite *un*comfortable. She had very clear eyes.

'Anyway, it'd be fun,' Japhet added lamely. He knew she could see through him.

'Yes; just another of your bits of fun-and-games. Well, I don't agree. You know everything you do only ends in trouble. Look at the rabbits. Whose fault was that, I should like to know?'

'Not mine!' shouted Japhet. 'Everyone always blames me!' And he stumped off to 'Scarface', Part Two; but Louisa knew he wouldn't be cross for long; he never was.

And the rabbits are not really important; it was just that Japhet had let all three of them out on the lawn one day, because he had read a piece in 'Pets' Corner' of his comic, saying all rabbits should have plenty of exercise. It was the family who had had most exercise, getting the rabbits back. Japhet's was next door, in Mrs Tucker's raspberries – and Mrs Tucker was deaf, so this took a lot of explaining. Louisa's ran into the field, and was caught after two hours with a fishing-net; and Rose's (it *would* be Rose's) nearly drowned in the ditch in front of the house, and was brought out plastered with black mud, which it shook all over the kitchen walls as their father carried it to dump it in the sink.

Their mother was washing-up at the time, so Japhet came in for an outburst of annoyance all round. But he did what he always did – just went away until people had calmed down.

Louisa had started Pakistan from the sea edge at the bottom, which was easy: blue sea, green land. But when she came to what she called the top end, there seemed to be a great muddle as to which bit was which. The land had changed to that dreary fawn, deepening to light tan, and there were red borders wriggling all over the place. So Louisa went to look at another map in her father's study; she liked to get things right.

This just shows what a mixture everything is: partly chance, partly the person. If Louisa had not been the kind of person she was, she might never have chanced to see what she saw in the study. And again, if she had not been Louisa, she might never have taken the chance and put it into action.

It lay on the table; simply a magazine, face downwards, the back page covered with advertisements. She wouldn't have looked, but a word seemed to jump out into her eye: the word 'Mushrooms'. She remembered her father saying that as soon as he'd heard an odd word he seemed straight away to hear or see it somewhere else: even their mother allowed that this was peculiar. Louisa felt a twitch of excitement to think that perhaps she had the same peculiarity.

'Grow Your Own Mushrooms,' she read; 'Why

7

Not?' Cautiously she thought there must be *some* reasons why not, otherwise everybody would do it, except those who really hated mushrooms.

'Send for Free Leaflet with all Information about this Fascinating and Profitable Hobby', said the advertisement; and there was the address of a farm in South East London. Louisa thought what a strange place for a farm; but she supposed anything could be called 'farm' where things were grown, and mushrooms, after all, could be grown in cellars.

She pondered carefully. In a way, she thought, it seems as if what with Japhet saying that and me seeing this, we must be *meant* to grow mushrooms. On the other hand, what an odd thing to be meant to do.

Then she thought about the mushroom man, and how she ought to be sorry for him even if he was sour; and what he would think of being presented with bags of mushrooms he hadn't had to work for; and how of course he wouldn't take them.

Then, for no reason at all, she thought of Rose's tooth. That had been put under the pillow, and according to custom was changed for a sixpence during the night. Rose still made out that the fairies did it, though she knew quite well they didn't. But all the same, Louisa had always liked the idea of presents under pillows, Easter eggs hidden in the garden, parcels left on doorsteps. For a sensible girl of fourteen, this may seem a little fanciful; but you can be sensible and still have fancies.

At the moment, Louisa had a strong fancy for doorsteps. Supposing they did grow mushrooms – couldn't they just leave some on the mushroom man's doorstep, without a word? Perhaps it's rather childish, thought Louisa, but it would be fun – even if we only did it once or twice. Creeping up to his cottage when he wasn't there; and then perhaps even buying the mushrooms back from him, and keeping a straight face.

Underneath all this, Louisa didn't cheat herself. She knew that really she did want to grow mushrooms. Not for the mushroom man particularly; just because she liked doing things; solid things, that showed results; new things, that needed organizing; and of course if they were also a help to anyone else, so much the better.

She decided to write to the mushroom farm. But – although she felt a little mean about this – she would not tell Japhet, yet. It might turn out to be much too difficult or expensive, and Japhet would never see these drawbacks. He would just rush hopefully on.

'Louisa, have you seen the frying-pan?' their mother was calling from the kitchen.

'No; Japhet had it outside.'

'And I told him not to! Japhet! Japhet!'

There was a mixture of noises then; the TV blaring as the sitting-room door opened; Japhet protesting;

9

their mother telling him to take the torch and go out and look.

Louisa found the top end of Pakistan in the other atlas; it looked much simpler, because it was all bright pink. She finished her own map there in the study, because she could still hear her mother and Japhet arguing.

'I've looked everywhere,' said Japhet. 'It's always me, isn't it?'

'What about the chicken-house?' A pause.

'*I* remember: I took it for the rabbits' oats!'

The back door banged; Louisa supposed that eventually there would be mushrooms for supper.

But she couldn't possibly know what they were going to do to her life – to all their lives – in the next few months. She carefully put her mapping-pen back in its cotton-wool, and took out an ordinary pen to answer that advertisement. It can be frightening to think how much good – and harm – an ordinary pen can do.

Chapter Two

'WE DON'T have homework,' said Japhet to the boy at the bus stop.

'We do,' said the boy, and put his nose closer into his Latin Grammar.

'Do you really want to go to Cambridge?'

'Yes. Why?'

'Nothing. My sister wants to go to Oxford. I think she's mad.'

'I thought you'd got two sisters,' said the boy, looking over the top of his spectacles.

'I have. The other one wants to be a singer, but she's only young. Besides, she can't sing.'

'How d'you know?'

'Well, how do you know anything?' said Japhet, surprised.

'Most things are a matter of opinion,' the boy remarked in an offhand voice. 'Except maths.' He put his hand over his book, looked up, shut his eyes and started muttering.

'The only opinion about Rose's singing,' said Japhet, 'is it's terrible. It keeps me awake at night. Anyway, it would, if I wanted to go to sleep. Here, have you got an exam or something?'

'No – (mutter, mutter) – only a test. But I've got to come top. This time I've just got to come top.' He screwed up his eyes and moved his lips faster than ever. Japhet decided that he was much worse than Louisa (whom, as a matter of fact, he secretly admired).

'Here's the bus,' said Japhet. 'I wonder if Podge has caught it today.'

'Is that the one you used to sit with at the back?'

'Yes; old Podge. He's been late three times this term already.'

'But you've only been back three days, haven't you?'

'Yes. Trust old Podge!' Japhet grinned approvingly.

The bus pulled up, and they climbed in, with bits of wet grass stuck to their shoes. Old Podge was actually there, beaming in the back seat, with his mouth full as usual.

'I say,' said the boy with the spectacles, as Japhet edged past him, 'how did you know?'

'What?'

'About Cambridge.'

'Now move along there, move along,' said the thin conductor, who found these school buses took it out of him. So Japhet only had time to say 'Oh, I just heard'; which was good, because he wouldn't have liked the boy to know that their mother had been talking about him.

'Me breakfast,' announced Podge. 'Want some?' He held out a paper bag containing a thick white sandwich.

'Egg,' he said. 'Go on.'

Japhet refused, going a little pink because as a matter of fact the sight of the sandwich made him feel slightly sick, and he was ashamed of this; it seemed mean. He was thinking of Podge's Mum, who always wore a woollen scarf tied round her head, with metal curlers sticking out in the front. Japhet quite liked her, although she was so fat, but the idea of her stuffing that cold, hard scrambled egg into that sandwich, and wearing those fur-edged slippers, somehow put him off.

Podge lived on the Council Estate a mile or so away; there were things there that Japhet envied, and things that made him uneasy.

'All the boys where Podge lives,' he had once told his mother, 'have great fat Mums and angry Dads.' This wasn't quite true, of course, but it was his general impression. On the other hand, Podge always had someone to play with: the roads in front of the houses there were full of children who were allowed to be out all day long, and even quite late in the evening. Very few cars went by, so it was safe to have bikes and roller-skates and push-carts, and even to play marbles in the middle of the road. Where Japhet lived, there was just the garden and the field, the common opposite, and Mrs Tucker's cottage next door. The road between the house and the common buzzed with fast cars going to the coast, so Japhet was only allowed to ride his bicycle in the field. But for all their differences, Podge was his best friend.

Miss McCormick had separated them twice already this term. She would probably have done the same on the other day too, but she was away at a funeral, and old Mr Glynn, who kept an eye on their class, never separated anybody. He just said, 'Now then, now then!' and let things be: things such as ink-soaked blotting-paper made into pellets and flipped at the girls; or somebody wearing a black plastic moustache in scripture; or two boys at the back binding and gagging Nigel Netherwell, so that he couldn't put up his hand and give all the right answers. Once a rabbit had been passed from desk to desk all round Mr Glynn's mental arithmetic class, and when it got to the front row he only said, 'Now then, now then, I should put that away if I were you,' but nobody did, so it just sat there.

In an odd way, Podge and Japhet felt more comfortable with Miss McCormick, who shouted at them whatever they did. You knew where you were with her: very low indeed. 'At least,' said Japhet, 'she can't get any worse.'

He spoke too soon. On this particular day, even though Podge was in time for prayers, she pounced on them before they had done anything at all. Podge had merely said out of the corner of his mouth, 'What's the idea, then, talking to the Grammar School?'

And Japhet had answered, 'Nothing; his father brings us mushrooms.'

To which Podge had hissed, 'Brings *whats*?' – and before Japhet could answer, Miss McCormick was striding between rows of faces that slowly turned round in amazement though they went on singing 'We plough the fields and scatter. . . .'

'All right!' whispered Miss McCormick venomously. 'All right: *Out*!' And with a terrible glare at Japhet, she took Podge by the collar and pushed him towards the door. Mr Glynn, who was in the way, politely moved aside; he looked concerned, and muttered, 'Poor little chap not well?' – which made Miss McCormick more furious than ever.

Perhaps the funeral upset her, Japhet suggested afterwards.

'I reckon it was that bit of cold pork,' said Podge.

'What bit?'

'I'd saved it up: well, you know I never sing the hymn anyway. She made me spit it out,' he added with disgust. '– And she called me names. I felt like saying to her, "My Mum could charge you for that pork and all." It was what was left over from my Dad's supper last night; she got it him for a treat. And then to go and have to spit it out!'

Japhet noticed with alarm that Podge was nearly in tears. He tried to change the subject.

'That boy in the bus,' he said, 'how old would you think he was?'

'Dunno,' sniffed Podge. 'Thirteen. Fourteen. My Mum wouldn't half be wild if she knew about that pork. Well, pork's expensive.' He was clearly brooding about it. The pork had been his fat Mum's way of trying to appease his angry Dad; Podge was indignant on her behalf. He was an only child, and very fond of his Mum.

'I must say, it's a bit much, not letting us sit together for the whole of the rest of this term,' said Japhet.

'Will I be glad when I leave this school,' sighed Podge, 'will I be glad!' For a naturally cheerful boy, he looked really depressed; his large pale face settled into a gloomy blank; even the tuft on the top of his head seemed to droop.

'Anyway, you're lucky,' said Japhet, 'you haven't even got to do the Eleven Plus.'

Japhet himself had been sent to the village school with this aim; he knew his parents wanted him to go to the Grammar, and the thought occasionally clouded his sky – but only occasionally. He didn't mind much where he went, as long as he had plenty of time to mess about and light bonfires. Neither Podge nor Podge's parents had the slightest desire for Podge to do anything but leave school as quickly as possible so that he could learn to be a butcher and work his way up.

'Well, I like meat,' said Podge, when Japhet suggested that it was a horrible thing to be. 'I think it's interesting, the different parts. I always go and choose the joint for Mum, Saturdays. She says it's good practice. Besides,' he added enthusiastically, 'at the pork butcher's they make their own sausages, and I might get a job doing that.'

'How dull,' said Japhet, who hated sausages.

'Dull?' Podge exclaimed in astonishment. 'Sausages dull? If it was arithmetic – but well, I mean, sausages is food, isn't it?'

And to Podge all food was interesting, so that was that. But Japhet liked him mainly because he was so good-tempered, and grinned so much, and was always ready to fool about in any lesson at all – and besides, he was generous, and wouldn't dream of eating the whole of anything if you happened to be looking.

But the day of the spat-out pork was a really black day for Podge. By the middle of the afternoon, Miss McCormick had separated him not only from Japhet but from everyone else as well; he had to pull his lonely desk out into the front and sit right up against the boiler fender, with nothing to look at but a coloured print of the Giant Carp which was plastered to the wall next to some Ancient Britons who had been there since last term. The desks were made to hold two, so Podge looked lonelier than ever. And all because he kindly passed somebody his gob-stopper when it had got to white.

Japhet sat moodily pitying Podge and disliking Miss McCormick. When it came to his turn to stand up and read aloud from *Gulliver's Travels*, he had lost the place; Miss McCormick grimly let him read a whole paragraph from a later chapter before she stopped him.

'I see,' she said. 'Congratulations. Wonderful. We didn't know we had a genius in the class, did we?' She looked round at the others, who smiled wanly or stared at their inkwells. '*We* are on chapter four, but he, no doubt, has read, marked, learned and inwardly digested that long ago. Dear me, yes. To say nothing of chapters five and six. Perhaps he can tell us what's in them, so that we may be spared the trouble of keeping our poor little places on PAGE THIRTY-THREE!' She let out the last words with a shriek and the slam of a ruler on Japhet's desk. His india-rubber leaped high into the air, and someone giggled.

'Who laughed?' demanded Miss McCormick. Silence. 'Well? Who thinks there's something funny?' By that time, nobody really did. She tapped the ruler on the palm of her hand for what seemed like minutes.

Podge gazed at the Giant Carp. Japhet concentrated on Miss McCormick's brown lace-up shoes. Nigel Netherwell looked virtuously at page thirty-three, ready to spring up and read if called upon. Everyone waited.

'Very well,' said Miss McCormick. 'Very well.' (People say that when they mean just the opposite, Japhet thought.) 'You don't want to learn. I don't particularly want to teach you. So we're even, aren't we? So we just sit here and look at each other until the bell goes. That's all. Just sit.' And she made the last word sound like a frightful punishment; which in fact, Japhet considered, it was – since there was no one he would less have liked to sit and look at, until any bell, than Miss McCormick. She was what he would call all brown. Eyes, hair, clothes – even her skin was brownish, except when she got red patches of rage round her neck.

Japhet sat and aimed bad wishes at Miss McCormick.

He was generally quite an affectionate and easy-going boy, but there were limits. By half-past three he was wishing his dog Oats could be there to snap her hard, from the back. By twenty-five to four he wanted her to be stung all over by bees. By twenty to, he had changed it to hornets. And by a quarter to, when the bell rang . . .

'If I was that man in "Scarface",' he said to Podge, 'I'd do her!'

'She'd only come round again,' said Podge. He was

lumbering hastily across the playground; he couldn't get out of that place quickly enough.

'I'd see she didn't. I'd give her the works. I wonder if she'll ever leave?' he added more realistically.

'No,' said Podge.

'Well, she'll have to, some time. Why can't she retire?'

'She's stuck,' said Podge. 'All teachers are.'

'Old Starbuck left,' said Japhet, unwilling to give up hope.

'Only because he got run over,' said Podge.

Japhet gave it up. Either way, there were limits. You couldn't really wish a person that sort of thing.

'There's the bus,' he said.

'I wonder if carp'd be all right fried,' Podge ruminated as they jolted along in the back seat.

Japhet said he didn't like fish anyway; but he'd rather talk about even a kipper than Miss McCormick. Podge smiled and started to give a list of what he would have for tea if he could absolutely choose.

Good old Podge.

Chapter Three

'EDITH'S COMING to stay,' their mother announced at breakfast.

'Who's Edith?' asked Japhet.

'Which Edith, what Edith?' Rose said in her Monday-morning voice.

'Don't be silly,' Louisa scolded, 'there's only one Edith. Edith Slater, of course.'

'Oh!' Japhet began to smile. 'You mean "Edith Slater, peeling a potater, Fell down the sink and came up later".' By the time he had come to the end of this, he could hardly speak for laughing; he nearly fell off his stool.

'That,' said Louisa, 'is not particularly funny.'

'You're not to say it when she comes,' their mother told him. 'You know she doesn't like it.'

'Tell me about the time when I did, and what she said – go on, do tell me again! How old was I?'

'Too young to know any better, I suppose,' said their mother.

'– And it was at tea, and I suddenly said "Edith Slater, peeling—"'

'Oh, not again,' protested Louisa.

'And what did she say, what did she say?' Japhet always hugged himself over this story. Besides, it was the first and only bit of poetry he had ever made up, and he still thought it was pretty good.

'She said you were a very rude and horrid little boy,' their mother sighed. Japhet tipped his stool back in delight.

'"Very rude and horrid",' he began in a tight squeak, but couldn't say more for laughing.

'I don't know what's so funny,' Louisa said. 'Anyway, she doesn't peel potatoes, she scrubs them; she told me so. To keep the vitamins in.'

'*I* don't know what you're talking about,' said Rose, 'at all.'

'You never do,' Louisa remarked, whereupon their mother had to pacify Rose quickly with a bowl of banana and sultanas and the top of the milk.

'When is she coming?' asked their father. Don't be surprised that he hadn't spoken before; talking at breakfast was a hope he had given up long ago.

Their mother rustled through the letter. 'She doesn't exactly say. You know she's always very vague. She might turn up at any time.'

'But who *is* she?' persisted Rose.

'That old school-friend of mine,' said their mother.

'She gave us those sweets made to look like pieces of bacon,' Japhet reminded her, 'and we had to throw them away.'

Louisa began to smile. 'She wears two skirts,' she said, 'and makes cheese sandwiches for birds.'

'Why—?' began Rose, but it was time for the school bus.

Indeed, as Louisa had remarked, there was only one Edith Slater. But we must wait for her arrival, as the family did, with the spare-room bed made up and the bowl for cooling tea put ready on the chest of drawers. It was Louisa who remembered the bowl – the white one with rosebuds – because she had once gone up with Edith Slater's early morning tea and had been asked to stand it in the cold water in the wash-basin, and wait until the thermometer had gone down to 85 degrees. Louisa had nearly missed the bus; since then, Edith Slater's bowl had been an institution. Japhet said, 'Why not make cold tea in the first place?' but Edith wouldn't hear of that.

So, with the rosebud china on a wool mat Rose had half-finished in kindergarten, and a bottle in the bed, the family waited for Edith to turn up at any time.

But Louisa had other things to think about. For instance: Rotted Horse-Manure, and Organic Fertilizers, and Horticultural Peat (three grades); and, most important of all, Mushroom Compost – described as 'Nature's own, ready for immediate spawning'.

The farm in South-East London had sent their promised details. Louisa took the letter into the bathroom, not wishing to be disturbed. There were two leaflets, one with prices and the other with instructions; the instruction one added, 'Five Good Reasons for ordering our Mushroom Compost'. Louisa read these carefully, and decided that the word 'our' should have been underlined: the people were simply out to show that their compost was better value than any other; they skipped the question whether you really wanted mushroom compost at all. But having read the leaflets twice, Louisa made up her mind that she did.

For one thing, she was a determined girl. Unlike Rose, she would never have left a wool mat half-finished. And what was more, she was struck by one immediate economy – 'Old Well-Rotted Horse-Manure'. The farm advertised this at a price of fourteen shillings one large sack; in that case, thought Louisa, Jo must be worth pounds and pounds. . . .

Jo was the pony they had on trust from a Society for the Protection of Old Ponies. This society found foster-homes for ponies who couldn't pull carts any more, or who were for some reason unwanted. Louisa's family had come to suspect that there was more than a cart behind nobody's wanting Jo: she was unrideable, unapproachable, had a nasty way of baring her teeth and rolling her eyes, kicked violently whenever she saw Oats the dog, and suffered from 'summer itch' – except,

24

as Rose pointed out, that it must be winter itch too, for Jo's coat was very mangy indeed all the year round. To see her from a distance, grazing in the field, you might have thought she was just another peaceful old pony; but those who knew her kept well away. Still, she did eat the thistly grass, which would have cost some pounds a year to have mowed. The family never cared to work out how many pounds it cost to buy Jo's oats in the winter; but apart from Louisa, they weren't much of a family for working things out. Besides, it did *look* nice to have a pony in the field. Visitors from town would beam and say, 'Oh, a pony!' and the family would beam back and say nothing.

But now Louisa did start to work out how much Jo would save them in the way of mushroom-growing: she reckoned that it might be a good third of the cost. Given 'Old Well-Rotted Horse-Manure', surely there was no need for other things such as Bone Meal, Hoof and Horn, or – she screwed up her face – Dried Blood? So that left just the spawn to be bought, and perhaps some peat. 'We supply sedge peat from seams of the finest deposits in the world,' said the advertisement; but when Louisa saw the prices she decided against peat. After all, mushrooms grew in fields, and no one supplied sedge peat there, so why worry? Just the spawn. Sixteen shillings a bag . . . Louisa looked thoughtful. This might be the time to take Japhet into her confidence after all.

Not that she was mean with money – far from it; in fact even now, in September, she was already calculating how much she could spend on Christmas presents. But after all, the mushrooms had been Japhet's idea, and she knew he had something in the plastic squirrel by his bed. Japhet had sent up to a breakfast-cereal company for this squirrel; it had cost him so much that he had nothing to put in it for weeks. But it turned out to be quite a good thing, as Louisa remarked, because once any money was inside, it lodged in the hind paws and was quite hard to get out again. So Japhet had saved more than he otherwise would.

In fact, he did manage to wheedle out half a crown, added to which he put half his that week's pocket-money, and Louisa supplied the rest of the sixteen shillings. Some of her Christmas presents would have to be home-made.

'Or you might give people mushrooms,' suggested Japhet, who was already thinking of setting up a stall with baskets by the roadside.

'For Christmas?' Louisa was doubtful. 'Anyway, we've got to grow them first. And anyway, what about the mushroom man? I thought the whole point—'

'Listen to this –' Japhet was studying the leaflets '– it says you have to keep them hot. It says "do not use an old-fashioned oil-heater, but a modern fumeless one however is quite suitable". What do they mean?'

'Electric fire, of course.' Louisa had gone into all this.

'What, in the garden?'

'No, the chicken-house. It says they can be grown anywhere under cover and it needn't be dark. Well, nobody ever goes to the chicken-house—'

'Nor does electricity,' Japhet pointed out.

'Electricity can go anywhere,' Louisa said firmly, 'as long as there's enough flex. All you need to do is join another piece on – we can use that old fire in the spare-room – and plug it into the ironing-point in the kitchen, and take it out through the window—'

'They won't like it being turned on all night,' said Japhet. He spoke from long experience of being told to turn things off, specially the TV.

'It won't be,' said Louisa, 'only when there's a frost. I'll see to that.'

This was good enough for Japhet; when Louisa said 'I'll see to that', you could be pretty sure all would be well. As for the mushroom man – even Louisa herself had to admit that she hadn't given him very much thought lately; she felt quite guilty about it until she remembered her father's motto, first things first: in this case, the first thing was the mushrooms.

' "Picking",' Japhet read out hopefully. ' "Mushrooms should be twisted and pulled, seeing that the stem and root come away with the—" '

'Never mind about picking,' Louisa interrupted him. 'I haven't even bought the postal-order yet. And they take six to eight weeks to grow, it says so.'

'What do? What postal-order?' Rose came in forlornly at the tail-end of the conversation, as usual.

'Don't tell her,' said Japhet.

'Oh, she might as well know,' Louisa sighed. Kindness mixed with common sense told her that Rose would find out sooner or later, and that sooner would mean less tears. So they told Rose, who only said in a perplexed way, 'But I don't like mushrooms.'

'What *you* like,' Louisa said, 'is not the point.'

'Then what is?' asked Rose, and they had to begin all over again.

But Louisa was really touched when, on the next morning, Rose laid a bloody tooth by her toast, and asked her mother if she could please have the sixpence now, straight away. She had pulled out the tooth herself; the sixpence she gave to Louisa as soon as their mother's back was turned – 'For you-know-what.' Louisa softened towards her; after all, blood was blood.

So the postal-order was sent off; and during the next few evenings they stealthily collected buckets of what Louisa hoped was Old Well-Rotted Horse-Manure from Jo's field, until the chicken-house was five inches deep with it all over. Louisa had seen five inches mentioned in one of the leaflets; it wasn't quite clear what this referred to, but she measured carefully with a ruler and hoped for the best.

'Won't it be lovely,' said Japhet, 'when this is all

covered with mushrooms? We might earn pounds!'

'We're still waiting for the spawn.' Louisa was privately wondering whether the postal-order had gone astray; but she need not have worried. The mushroom spawn arrived by the tea-time post on the following day; so did Miss Edith Slater.

Chapter Four

'ANYWAY,' sighed their mother, 'she's the only person who ever takes Oats out for a walk.'

'You mean he takes her,' said Rose. 'He goes for his own walks.'

Certainly Oats must have had a charmed life; he roamed that dangerous road at will, and always came back.

'But he likes being taken,' Japhet said. 'He smiles.'

'Who wouldn't smile,' said Louisa, 'at Edith?'

'Edith wouldn't,' said Rose, who sometimes hit the nail on the head. Their mother told them that was enough, and gave their father a straight look.

'If only she *would* peel a potater—' he began; but realized that he ought not to criticize a visitor in front of the children.

'She does make her bed,' said their mother rather despondently. The trouble was, Edith had been with them for over a week and showed no sign of leaving. They did like to have her, and she was not at all a nuisance really, but neither was she very much help.

'It's not that she's unwilling,' said their mother, 'she just doesn't see things.'

This, though, had its advantages: for instance, when Edith came down to Saturday breakfast after ten o'clock, she didn't even see what might by then be on the kitchen table, such as a wellington boot, a rabbit hutch or a few apple cores. She simply went on placidly and seriously eating the mixture of cream cheese and marmalade and raw porridge she had made for herself the night before. It was just like home, she said. All the same, it irritated their father to see their mother washing-up while Edith sat among the birds.

'Why *do* you make them cheese sandwiches?' Rose had asked.

'So that they all get their proper vitamins,' replied Edith Slater. 'Otherwise some might have nothing but starch and the wily ones take all the protein. Which would be bad.' And she went on grating old cheese all over the kitchen tablecloth; bits of it leaped into the fruit salad their mother had made for lunch; Louisa often found shreds in the folds of her exercise books.

On this particular Saturday morning, their father was determined that Edith should do her bit. So he picked the very last of the runner beans, and put her in the late September sunlight, under a yellowing apple tree, with a bowl and a knife and a newspaper and a chair and a table.

'Now, Edith, you're all right, aren't you?' he said, and marched off to chop wood.

Half an hour later, Louisa found the table deserted, the beans apparently untouched; then she saw Edith's head bobbing among the bean-sticks in the vegetable garden.

'Whatever are you doing, Edith?'

Edith Slater looked mildly guilty. 'I was giving him another chance,' she said. He was a grub; she was coaxing him back on to a leaf.

'Really,' Louisa told her mother as she finished the last bean, 'Edith is hopeless! It's all very well to be an animal-lover—'

'Grubs count as animals,' said Japhet. He sometimes collected them; besides, he thought the family was a little hard on Edith, who had spent the whole of the previous evening re-stuffing his limp bear. It wouldn't sit down now, but it reminded Japhet of Podge; and he was always impressed by kindness.

'Oh well, she's a spinster,' their father said, as if that explained everything. Of course Rose had to ask, 'What's a spinster?'

'An unmarried female,' said Louisa. 'You're one.'

'Well, so are you—' Rose began indignantly.

'The only trouble with Edith,' their mother put in, 'is that she's not very practical.'

'Does she really wear two skirts?' Japhet asked.

'That was only once, when it was very cold. Thin

people feel the cold; besides, she'd only brought a knitting-bag. By the way, has anybody seen that electric fire out of the spare-room? She'll be wanting it now the nights are turning chilly.'

Japhet and Louisa looked at each other; here was a complication. That electric fire was in fact on a box in the chicken-house, with some twenty yards of flex wound round it, ready. Louisa had bought the cheapest flex with the last of her money; Japhet had taken off the plug and joined the new flex on by twisting it round the old and covering the place with sticky tape. He had put back the plug – correctly, he hoped. They hadn't tried it out yet: the spawn had only been in a few days, and the nights, Louisa said, were not frosty. But there was no doubt that they would be – and then, if Edith Slater stayed, how were they to keep the temperature of the mushrooms up to sixty degrees Fahrenheit?

'Sixty is not essential, it says,' Louisa muttered over the leaflet, 'but below fifty they just lie dormant.'

'What's dormant?' asked Rose.

'Asleep,' said Louisa. 'Don't interrupt, I must think.'

It would not be simple, she told them that evening, but it would have to be done.

'Isn't there another fire somewhere?' Japhet asked. He was not at all pleased at the idea of fixing and unfixing that plug and flex every time.

'No,' said Louisa, 'there isn't.'

'But how are we to get it out of her room? She'll want it for going to bed.'

'Rose,' said Louisa, 'will have to do that.'

'Shall I?' Rose looked startled. 'How?'

'Call,' said Louisa.

'Call what? When? Why?'

'Well, you often do. Only this time you won't call downstairs, you'll just call Edith. She's kind, she's sure to come. And she goes to bed before the others. And your room's next to hers, so you'll hear her switch off the fire. Then you call. And while she's in with you, either Japhet or I will go and get the fire. She's so absent-minded, she probably won't notice – specially if you make a long enough fuss.'

'Fuss what about?' complained Rose.

'Knowing you, anything,' snapped Louisa. 'Considering you call for something or other practically every night, surely you can think of *some* fuss.'

'Every night?' Rose looked doubtful.

'No, only when there's a frost. I'll tell you; I shall listen to the forecasts.'

'But if there are a lot of frosts, I might run out of fusses,' said Rose.

'The forecasts are no good,' Japhet added. Louisa was exasperated with them both.

'Here am I,' she said, 'doing my best, and what do I get? Nothing but arguments. You can do it once, at any rate,' she told Rose, 'and see how it goes. And you'd better be ready – it might be tonight. These fine September days often turn to frost.' That was what Mr Root, the occasional gardener, always said.

'If she does it often enough,' Japhet suggested hopefully, 'Edith might get fed up and go home.' He did like Edith, but the electric fire seemed more important.

'Anyway,' Louisa said briskly, 'that's fixed. Then I shall take the fire to my room, and Japhet can do the flex and plug, and as soon as they're all in bed I'll creep down and fix it up.'

'Why you?' Japhet objected. 'Why should you have all the fun?'

'Because I'm the oldest.'

'It's not fair—' began Rose; then her expression changed. 'If you don't let me come down and help,' she said, 'I shan't call.'

'And I shan't do the plug,' said Japhet.

Louisa looked at them; they glared back.

'I can perfectly well change the plug myself, if it comes to that,' she said loftily. 'And I suppose –' with some hesitation –'I could lure Edith out of her room somehow.'

'If you don't let me come down and be in it,' said Rose, 'I shall tell them what you're doing!' She knew this would be mean, but it was her last resort. There were tears in her eyes; she had so often been left out because she was the youngest. 'After all, I did pull out a tooth,' she said.

Louisa was beaten. 'All right, all right. In that case, we'd better organize exactly who's going to do what . . .'

Organizing anything generally made her feel better – but this time she was still vaguely uneasy; she couldn't have said why. After all, if she called Rose, and Rose called Edith, and Edith came out, and Japhet 'did' the fire, and they waited until their parents were in bed, and Louisa herself came down first to give Oats a biscuit so that he wouldn't bark . . .

It all went according to plan. Louisa had secretly exulted when she heard the radio announce 'Frost warning'; another mild night would have been an anti-climax. She went up and told Rose, in a stage-whisper, 'Tonight!' adding, 'For goodness' sake don't go to sleep!'

Rose sat bolt upright, quietly singing hymns, until she heard Edith switch off her fire. Then she called.

'Will you tell me about when you were a little girl? Please?'

Edith sat on the end of the bed, blew her nose on a paper tissue and began. She loved to talk about the past.

An hour later, Louisa gently rapped on Rose's door. The grown-ups were all snoring; Japhet stood on the landing nearly in stitches at the sound; he thought the very word 'snore' was funny, and three lots going on at the same time, on different notes, was almost more than he could bear.

With only a few creaks, they proceeded downstairs; Louisa first, carrying the fire and Oats's biscuit; Rose next, holding up the coil of flex, and Japhet last with the plug end.

Oats showed his surprise by refusing to eat the biscuit, but he didn't bark. What he did want to do was to join in; he rushed out of the back door after Louisa.

'He thinks he's going for a walk!' grinned Rose, following.

Japhet passed the fire to them through the window. He was to plug it in and switch on after he had counted a hundred; meanwhile, Louisa would put the fire in the chicken-house while Rose guided the flex on its way in the dark so that it didn't catch on to any rose bushes or other obstacles.

Silence. Japhet counted. Louisa stumbled and wished she had remembered to put on her boots; too late now. If her slippers were messy she would have to clean them before breakfast.

Rose shivered, in her blue dressing-gown, on what they pleased to call 'the terrace' outside the kitchen window. This was just an oblong of concrete slabs, good for hop-scotch; Louisa had tried to improve it by putting a tub of nasturtiums in a corner, but they were too often topped with rain-soaked toffee-papers or little strips of spent caps.

The thin flex sped through Rose's fingers; she scampered to and fro, helping it over the low stone ledge that bordered the terrace. Oats scampered with her, more and more excited.

Japhet counted. Sixty-nine, seventy, seventy-one. . . .

Louisa was carefully tilting the fire towards the centre of the chicken-house.

. . . Seventy-nine, eighty. . . . Surely she must be ready by now? Japhet felt like a man about to release a bomb. He put his hand on the switch. He heard a creak overhead in his parents' room; but it was only his father turning over in bed.

Louisa shone the torch round the chicken-house, and waited. In a few moments, she judged, the fire would come on and there would be a comforting red glow, and those mushrooms would surely feel it and respond. Of course she would have to take the fire in again in the morning before anyone saw it; but she had an alarm clock; she would do that part of the operation alone. She was just working out how many hours' sleep she would actually have. . . .

A flash. An explosion. A blood-curdling yelp. Then dead silence.

'What happened?' Louisa and Japhet arrived on the terrace at the same time.

There, stretched out with the flex in his mouth, lay Oats, quite still. The body in the dark beside him was Rose.

Chapter Five

'How often have I told you never to tamper with electricity?'

'She might have been killed!'

'Of all the stupid, dangerous things—'

'You, at least, ought to have known better, Louisa.'

'So ought Japhet. The boy's a fool. Look at this join, just look at it!'

'He must have bitten it where the sticky tape—' began Japhet.

'I don't care where he bit it, you'd no business to have the fire at all.'

And so it went on. Their parents, in dressing-gowns, poured out their fright in the form of angry words upon Japhet and Louisa. Upstairs, Rose lay in bed as white as a sheet, but, thank goodness, alive. She had had a shock through Oats, when she tried to pull him away from the flex; but she had come round when they carried her indoors. Their mother made tea, trembling, and took it up.

'Is Oats all right?' asked Rose.

'Now don't worry; just drink this. Fancy going out there in the middle of the night, with a frost too!'

'I'm sorry,' said Rose, 'but it was the frost that made me.'

'Don't you ever, ever do such a thing again.'

'No, but *is* Oats all right?'

'Daddy'll see to Oats. I want you to drink this up and go to sleep.'

Their mother couldn't scold Rose any more; it was such a relief that she was safe. Besides, she had been led into it by the others, and it was always the same: if they did anything dangerous, Rose was surely the one who would have the accident. They often grumbled that she came off lightly because of this; but now even Japhet was shaken. And there was the terrible question of Oats.

No, Oats was not all right. Their father had switched off the current and pulled the flex out of the stiff half-opened mouth; then he carried the dog in to his basket. Japhet and Louisa looked on with horror. Oats was stretched in a nasty, peculiar position; his head back, his hind legs drawn up, his eyes open but rolled agonizingly sideways.

'Oh, do ring up the vet,' begged Louisa, 'please do!'

'It's after midnight.'

'Can you feel his heart?' Japhet asked. 'Look – I think I saw his paw twitch!'

'No, I kicked the basket. Louisa, get an old rug.'

'Please, please ring the vet. After all, it's the same as a doctor.'

'Do as I say; get an old rug.'

'What for?' Japhet asked.

'A very old one; or that sack in the garage.'

'Sack?' Louisa stopped dead, feeling sick.

'Yes, and hurry up. We can't leave him here all night.'

'But where are you going to put him?'

'Outside until the morning.'

'Outside? But it's cold, it's frosty, there's a mist—'

'That won't matter,' said their father, adding grimly, 'not now.'

'What do you mean?' But Louisa and Japhet both knew. Even Japhet went pale.

'I mean he's dead.'

Louisa burst into tears; her mother came down and found her bent on a stool sobbing into the tablecloth; she gave her a handkerchief out of the boiler cupboard, where they were kept with Ryvita and salt and other things. Japhet stared at Oats and struggled between a terrible fascinated interest and an equally terrible lump in his throat. The dog did look queer; the more you gazed, the less he seemed to be their own Oats. He had turned into a nightmare dog. It was that twist at the side of his mouth. . . . Japhet went away to be sick.

'Well, hurry up,' said their father, 'I'll have to wrap him up in something. And I'm certainly nct coming

St. HELEN'S SCHOOL
LIBRARY

down to have porridge with a dead dog.' Louisa glanced at him, and saw him turn away. She knew that if he seemed heartless, it was only because he really did care, and hated to show his feelings. After all, it was her father who had brought Oats in the first place; her father who had given him a bath when he had fallen into the black ditch; her father who had taken that thorn out of his paw, and who always took him out last thing at night; her father whom Oats had welcomed home with the most joyful bark, the happiest beaming muzzle. . . .

Louisa cried herself to sleep. But being Louisa, she didn't only cry: she also thought. First, about those wretched mushrooms. Whatever had possessed her to undertake such a scheme? She felt all the worse because she knew she had done it, really, much more for the fun than for the mushroom man. That bag on the doorstep business was just a sentimental fancy; an excuse. She was too honest to deny it. And now poor Oats; Oats who had done no harm; who had never been taken out for proper walks; who had rushed into the dark that night so happily, with such hope and trust. She thought, too, of course, about Rose; but not with such feeling. After all, Rose had survived, and would no doubt swank horribly at school about having had an electric shock.

But something must be done to make up for it all. Louisa lay in the dark, wet and desperate: what could she possibly do to relieve her guilt just a little? Not go on trying to grow mushrooms, that was certain. She never wanted to see a mushroom again, let alone eat one. A single forlorn idea occurred to her – but it was better than nothing. She could offer the mushroom man the spawn and manure, free: it would at least get rid of the beastly stuff, and prove that she was not absolutely heartless and useless. Yes, that was what she would do. Then she thought of Oats's expectant eyes – so often disappointed – and the way his tail slowly beat the floor when he lay by the fire and you mentioned his name, and how he loved to bounce among the heather if you took him for a picnic. It was unbearable, and she went to sleep on a damp pillow, in sheer despair.

As for Edith Slater – she was the one person in the house who had a completely peaceful night. She slept soundly throughout the whole affair, dreaming of wild canaries.

But on the next day, Edith was in mourning with the rest of them. Rose stayed in bed; the others went gloomily to school. The cream cheese and marmalade were untouched.

Louisa ploughed heavy-hearted through Latin and maths and a double science period; she was not even much cheered to be told that she had won last year's form prize. She felt she didn't deserve to win anything.

Japhet was unusually good and quiet; even Podge couldn't make him smile.

'There's other dogs.'

'They wouldn't be Oats.'

'Pity it wasn't *her*,' said Podge, meaning Miss McCormick. 'But I reckon she'd go and come round,' he added hopelessly. 'By the way, have you thought of anything yet? I wish she'd go to Russia or get married or something. But people like her never do.'

Japhet was too low even to consider this; Podge tried again.

'We've had two dogs,' he said. 'One got run over and the other had to be put away. I mean it shows there *is* other dogs.'

'Why did it have to be put away?'

'Overeating. He cost too much, and he was fat enough to burst; so Mum had him put away before he did. She said it was kinder.'

'Why didn't you give him less?'

'You couldn't. He was up on the table all the time, taking it. One tea-time he ate both my fried eggs before I had a chance, chips and all. Both! If he wasn't eating he was begging; my Mum said it got on her nerves. And she was dead scared he'd burst. That or poison himself. So she says no more dogs.'

All this only made Japhet feel worse; he thought Podge's people weren't really fit to have dogs at all; but he said nothing.

'What about a cat, then?' Podge suggested. 'Our next-door neighbour has ever so many kittens, all colours; they drown them in a bucket; you could have one for nothing.'

Japhet turned away; he had never felt so lonely or so distant from the well-meaning Podge. Even Miss McCormick, that afternoon, asked him if he would like to go home; his face was hardly pink at all, and he had given away all his packed lunch. But no; he didn't want to go home to that bundle of sacking in the chicken-house. He didn't want to go anywhere. He only wanted to see Oats wag his tail again; and he never would.

Edith Slater had a sad day, too. Most of it she spent going to and from the chicken-house, where she had gently laid Oat's head on a pillow of straw.

When Louisa came home from school, she could bear it no longer. She wandered about eating biscuits until she realized that she absolutely must *do* something – and not just homework. She would go and ask the mushroom man if he wanted that spawn, and whether he could come and fetch it. A feeble enough gesture, perhaps, but at least it would take her out of that house where every eye seemed to reproach her, and the dish still lay beside the empty basket.

'Mind you're back well before dark,' her mother said; but it was only just after five, and the mushroom man's cottage was barely half a mile away.

The early October evening was pink and still; there was already a moon, and the mist had begun to settle on the hills. Louisa looked at the wonderful sky where the sun would soon set, and thought she had never been so miserable.

Chapter Six

THE cottage lay low, between a stream and the bank of a one-track railway. It must be very damp here in winter, Louisa thought. A light showed in a downstairs window; she went round to the back and knocked with her hand on the brown door; there was no bell. She noticed a huge pink shell lying on the doorstep, which was also painted brown.

'Yes?' The boy with glasses stood there, blinking. She recognized him from the bus stop; but he looked different now. No jacket or tie – and he was wearing a large flowered apron, with a bib that crossed over at the back. He peered out of the light at where she stood in the near-dusk.

'Is your father in?'

'No, he's working late this week. Why?'

'I wondered if he'd like some mushroom spawn. We want to give some away.'

'He's stopped growing them.'

'Oh.' Louisa looked past him into the narrow hall,

where there were old raincoats hanging, and a broom stuck out just where someone might trip over it. She noticed that the boy had a book in his hand.

'They didn't pay. Good evening.'

But Louisa was not to be put off so easily. 'Still, if he didn't have to pay for the stuff in the first place,' she said, '—and we do so want to get rid of it.'

'Why?'

'Oh, there's nothing actually wrong with it – only it has, well, unhappy memories.'

Normally she wouldn't have dreamed of saying such a thing; but she was tired and wretched.

'*Memoriae infelicae*,' said the boy. 'That's Latin.'

'I know. But shouldn't it be infeli*ces*?' She looked the boy straight in the eye; that'll take him down a peg, she thought, little show-off.

Now it was the boy who looked wretched. 'Oh dear,' he said, 'oh dear yes, I think you're right.' He wiped a hand on the apron and began thumbing through the book.

'Never mind, what does it matter? Can I come in and wait for your father?'

'But it does matter, very much. Latin's my worst subject; oh dear, I'll never pass.'

'I'm not much good either,' said Louisa comfortingly, 'but I'm worse at maths.'

'Well, you're a girl.' This annoyed Louisa so much that she decided to teach him quite a different sort of lesson; she marched right past him into the hall, and said thank you, she would like to wait.

He followed her into the kitchen.

'I didn't mean to be rude—' he began.

'You shouldn't go about telling people they're girls.'

'Well, you are.'

'I don't wish to be reminded of it,' said Louisa with dignity. 'Anyway, you look a bit girlish yourself, at the moment.' But the instant she had said that, she regretted it.

The kitchen struck her at once with a single impression: sad. Pitiful, lonely and sad. Looking round, she sorted out the reasons why this should be so; she was quick at noticing details.

There was a naked light bulb over a scrubbed wooden table; the electricity stared at the pink light from outside, which only came in through one small window over the sink: a wretched kind of sink, made of old fawn porcelain, with cracks. On the table was a jamjar containing a spray of artificial lilac, rather dusty. There was also half a loaf, a packet of butter and a very small sausage on a very large plate. On the mantelpiece were two of last year's Christmas cards, tinselled ones, and several school-books. Another book was propped open on the draining-board, against a pile of saucepans. The tiled floor was half-wet; a bucket and mop stood there, and two pairs of shabby shoes had been carefully put up on the dresser out of the way;

they lay between a crinoline tea-cosy and a bottle of ink. There were no pictures, only a calendar with the name of a shop across the top, and a Remembrance Day poppy twisted round the string.

The boy in his flowered apron looked the saddest sight of all; no wonder he swanks a bit, Louisa thought; he has something to make up for.

'What were you doing?'

'Only the floor. And my Latin. And having tea.'

'All at once? Is that your tea?'

'Yes, why?'

'Oh, nothing.' She was thinking that her mother wouldn't have considered one sausage and white bread a very healthy tea; but then, her mother had what her father called a 'thing' about brown bread, and fruit, and cheese, though she didn't go to such lengths as Edith Slater, who was apt to make mud-coloured nut rissoles.

'Dad has the same, when he comes in. I keep his hot.'

There was a covered plate over a saucepan on the gas stove.

'But do you mean you have to do the housework?'

'Who else would?'

He said it quite simply, not at all resentful; he just accepted this as his way of life. Louisa felt very sorry for him.

'I'll finish the floor, if you like,' she said, 'while you do your Latin.'

After a very little persuasion, he agreed; he was clearly glad – he had yet another test the next day. He sat with his feet up on the table while Louisa mopped round him. Silence, except for the slosh of the mop, the simmering of the saucepan and the turning-over of pages.

'Have you finished? I'll wash-up your plate.'

'It's not washing-up day.' She looked surprised, so he explained, 'We only wash-up twice a week. Mondays and Fridays.'

Indeed, the sink was full of dirty dishes – a sight that always depressed Louisa very much, and she was depressed enough already.

'I'll do them,' she said, 'if you don't mind.'

'*I* don't mind. It's Dad. Well, he's been doing it Mondays and Fridays ever since—' he stopped short.

'What's your name?' Louisa asked, to change the subject.

'David.'

'I don't even know your surname. We just call your father the mushroom man.'

'Well he isn't now. It's Browne, with an "e".'

'That's funny; mine's Brown without an "e". It's rather distinguished to have an "e",' she added. Somehow the 'e' comforted her; it made up a little for the kitchen. On the other hand, fancy having an 'e' and living like that. He might really be a member of some noble family, come down in the world; he might even be a long-lost cousin, and hers the family which had mislaid the 'e'; they were always mislaying something. Suppose . . . but she decided she had better curb her imagination and get on with the washing-up. Everything was caked with dried potato; through the little window she could see across the common where the clouds were now orange and the ground-mist white. A stray dog ran by; if only it were Oats! She scrubbed and scraped and her tears fell into the sink. Luckily, the boy was too deep in maths to notice.

'What's going on? What do you think *you're* up to?'

The mushroom man – we shall now have to call him Mr Browne – stood in the doorway in his boots and his cap, with a very sour and suspicious look on his face. Louisa tried to explain.

'Very kind, I'm sure,' said Mr Browne, 'but this is Wednesday. We've enough plates to last till Friday, and as for the spawn, I wouldn't touch it. So you'd better clear out, hadn't you?'

'She helped me with my Latin,' said David.

'Oh. Well, Latin's one thing, washing-up's another. If I needed help, I'd get it.'

'Would you?' Louisa looked at him; she felt that somewhere underneath this sourness was a kind of pride; the pride of a Browne with an 'e', who didn't like to be caught out in a neglected kitchen. He looked at her too, more closely.

'Been crying?'

'Of course not.'

'Anything wrong?'

'Nothing. Nothing at all. I'll go home now.' It was the turn of the Browns without the 'e' to have a little pride; she took up her blazer with quite an air. To her surprise, he helped her on with it.

'Sorry if I was a bit short,' he said. 'I didn't mean to be what you might call ungrateful. And if you helped the boy with his Latin . . . it's a teaser, the Latin; I never learnt it myself. Only I haven't washed-up of a Wednesday for near on ten years; I suppose we get set in our ways.'

She said good-bye and walked thoughtfully home. What was she to make of him? In books, people were generally either good or bad; she had been prepared to write him off as bad – but there was something disturbing about the way he had seemed to relent at the end; about his uprightness and his sudden, unsmiling politeness. She wondered if smiling was a thing he hadn't done for ten years, either.

But as soon as she was within sight of home, vague wonder was wiped out. Something had happened. She felt it directly she saw the house with every light on from bedroom to hall.

'He moved!' squeaked Edith Slater. 'That dog moved!'

The family rushed out to the chicken-house; Japhet went back to unhook the torch from behind the door under the stairs, and shone it into the face – yes, into the eyes of Oats. And the eyes blinked.

'It's impossible,' said their father.

'He's alive, he's alive!'

'Good old Oats!'

'For heavens' sake,' said their mother, 'bring him indoors, and call the vet at once.'

Louisa found the house in an uproar. Rose and Japhet were tearing up and down stairs with old pillows, dolls' eiderdowns and rubber balls. Japhet even put his bear in Oats's basket, to cheer him up. The vet, their mother said, was on his way.

'It's a miracle!' sighed Edith Slater. 'And to think, if I hadn't been keeping watch . . .'

More than ever before, Oats seemed to be a dog with not nine, but nine-hundred and ninety-nine lives, and all of them toughly charmed.

'And to think he's a mongrel!' Japhet was particularly pleased about this. 'I bet a thorough-bred would have died; I bet a poodle would've; but not Oats! He's a good boy – aren't you, Oats, you're a clever boy; yes, you wouldn't go and die, no you wouldn't . . .'

Japhet had to be pulled away; Oats was still in no fit state to be hugged.

'I ought to have sent for the vet before,' said their

father, 'but I was so certain. His heart had stopped, I'm sure of it. It's extraordinary.'

The vet thought so too, when he arrived and heard the story. He pretended not to be quite so much amazed as he was, but they all felt that Oats would go down in history as the dog who came to life.

'Mind you, you'll have to keep him quiet,' said the vet, 'for a day or two, at least. And that mouth – I'm afraid there's a bit of paralysis there.' Oats looked as if he was smiling on one side only; but his eyes were bright and his tail gave a weak thump against the side of the basket.

'We ought to have a party,' said Louisa, 'to celebrate.'

'With a birthday cake.'

'Bone,' said Rose.

'*Re*-birthday,' Louisa improved.

'I'm afraid he won't be able to tackle a bone yet awhile,' said the vet, but he accepted a cup of tea himself.

So they all sat round the kitchen table, and it ended up in baked beans and swiss roll and tomato soup and bananas and a tin of peaches and bacon and egg and sardines and chocolate biscuits. . . . Their mother even found a box of crackers left over from last year, and they finished up wearing paper hats; Oats had Rose's best pink party ribbon tied to his collar. Their father kept giving the vet more cider, and they both seemed contented; their mother made cocoa for everyone else, and thought whatever happened in the night would just have to happen; Oats was worth it – or rather, having the children happy again was.

It was a rowdy evening – they even sang *For He's a Jolly Good Fellow* round Oats's basket, and Oats looked up and gave them a one-sided smile.

But in the middle of this, Louisa stopped. Why did she suddenly want to cry again? Here was light, and noise, and food, and people. What more do you need?

She had a vision of an owl-like boy in an apron. And of a tall, thin, unsmiling man. And of a lonely kitchen with artificial lilac and washing-up on Friday.

'Is he coming for it?' asked Japhet before they went to bed. He didn't really care now, one way or the other; Oats was the point. All the same, being an ever-hopeful boy, he had filled a brown paper bag with spawn from the chicken-house and stuffed it into the tea-pot in his bedroom. You never knew.

'No,' said Louisa. 'No. What that man needs is not mushrooms. What he needs—' she paused. The litter of red crêpe cracker-paper, the warmth, the echo of noise, the sight of Oats in his basket, the blue and white china that would be clean for breakfast by morning – everything joined to make her quite sure. 'What he needs,' she repeated, 'is not mushrooms at all. He needs *a wife*!'

Japhet shrugged and went to bed; he wasn't interested.

Rose, awkward as usual, said, 'What sort of wife?'

and was whipped off to the bath.

Edith Slater asked who wanted what, but wouldn't have listened to the answer, anyway; she was too much wrapped up in Oats.

And Oats just gave his one-sided smile – which didn't mean anything; he was to give it all the time for the rest of his life.

Louisa decided that she might as well forget the idea; after all, you couldn't write up and answer advertisements for wives. But sometimes ideas we forget don't forget us – or they come back in unexpected ways. Meanwhile, the house slept happily that night; and as happy as anyone was Edith Slater, who was to stay for another week 'to see Oats round the corner' – and, incidentally, to sit in for their parents on the following Saturday.

'It's not often we get asked out to dinner,' said their father, 'and still less often we can go. We might as well make use of her while we can.' Their mother hesitated; she wasn't sure if Edith could cope. If she had known what Edith would have to cope *with*, she would not have gone at all – but then, if we could see into the future, there would be no stories to tell.

Chapter Seven

Japhet and Podge sat in the bus comparing fireworks. Japhet's father had said that it was illegal to buy them yourself until you were thirteen; but the shop where they went didn't seem to know this law. Anyway, Podge had a Flying Saucer, two Crack Pots, a Sandstorm, a Dragon's Fire, a Mount Etna and a number of bangers, including a Mighty Atom, a Barrier Breaker, a Blaster and some Block Busters. Japhet had fewer – because of the half-crown he had spent on those mushrooms. But he had found a way to make them go further: you just cut open one end and tipped the powder out in little heaps wherever you wanted it, and lit each heap separately. This didn't make much of a show in the way of stars or coloured lights, but it did produce a series of quite good bangs. He had tried it along the garden path the night before, and Edith Slater had ticked him off for upsetting Oats.

The boy with the glasses was in the seat just in front of them; he glanced over his shoulder at the row of bright pink, green and blue cylinders and cones in Japhet's case-lid, and looked away with what they took to be a superior air.

Podge nudged Japhet. 'Look at old snooty,' he said. 'Bet he thinks his-self too big for these. He wouldn't half jump if one went off!'

Japhet eyed the back of the boy's neck, bent as usual over some homework. It annoyed Japhet that anyone should do homework *both* ways on the bus. And once, long ago, Podge had kindly asked the boy, 'Want a read of my comic?' and had been told in a cool way, 'No thanks, I've got French,' which Podge thought was slightly insulting and affected. 'Oh dear, oh lah-di-dah!' Podge had said, and had never spoken to the boy again.

There was something very tempting about that neck. The way it was so industriously bent; and the Grammar School cap set so very straight.

'Wouldn't it be funny if his cap went off?' whispered Japhet.

'How?'

Japhet opened the end of a firework.

'Go on – I dare you!' said Podge.

Japhet looked round; no one else on the bus was paying any attention; the conductor was somewhere up at the front, struggling between the wedged passengers with their satchels or shopping baskets or umbrellas.

'Just a tiny speck wouldn't hurt, would it?' he said doubtfully.

'Go on!' urged Podge.

'All right. Where?'

'Right on top of his loaf. On the button.'

Japhet tipped a little grey powder on to the offending cap.

'Dead centre!' Podge hugged himself.

'Shut the case,' said Japhet, 'and be looking out of the window.'

'I dare you to light a match,' said Podge.

'Somebody'd see,' said Japhet. 'Anyway, I haven't got one.'

'What's the point, then?'

'Nothing, only it's funny.' Having rather more imagination than Podge, Japhet was satisfied with the mere idea of the boy's going about with a *possible* explosion on top of his cap – he asked no more.

But sometimes we get more than we ask for.

There was a notice in the bus: 'Smokers are Requested to Occupy Rear Seats'. Podge and Japhet had never yet smoked, but they always occupied these seats because they were farthest away from the conductor.

Now between their seat and David's stood a man with a pipe. And the pipe had gone out. And the man was trying to relight it. And at that moment the bus gave a terrific jerk, because somebody had tried to stop it at a place that was not really a stop.

The man with the pipe lurched forward, said 'Pardon' to a woman with a bunch of red beech-leaves that spiked him in the eye – and dropped his latest match.

There was a deafening bang. At least, it seemed deafening in that crammed bus. And a shower of sparks, and a sharp smell, and some shrieks. The brakes screeched and the bus pulled to a standstill.

Smoke was coming out of the top of David's cap and he had his hand up to his face. To Japhet's horror, there was a small trickle of blood. Everybody was craning round, everybody was talking and asking and exclaiming, in the way people do when they are pretending not to have been frightened.

'Who done that?' yelled the conductor. He pushed and elbowed his way towards the back. 'Come on then, who done it?'

'My glasses are broken,' said David. For a dreadful moment Japhet thought of glass in eyes, of blindness, of himself in court, in prison. . . .

But no, the boy had a small scratch on the bridge of his nose; the frame of his glasses was neatly split into two halves.

'Look out,' said Podge, 'your cap's on fire!' And he snatched the smoking object and threw it out of the window; it landed in a blackberry-bush.

'Now look what you've done!' said David.

'What the so-and-so do you lot think you're playing at?' The conductor was grey with fury.

'Well, he was on fire,' said Podge. 'You don't want somebody in the bus on fire, do you?'

'And who put him on fire?' The conductor glared into Podge's face. 'You tell me that, then. Who done it?'

'He just went off,' said Japhet.

'None of your lip. Here, you know something about this, don't you? Let's have a look in that case.'

'It's only my lunch.'

'I dropped a match,' confessed the man with the pipe. 'But only an ordinary one. Nothing explosive.'

By now all the other passengers had stopped talking; Japhet felt worse and worse.

'Lunch! I'll give you lunch! Come on, open up.'

'I don't mind the cap so much,' said David. 'It's my glasses.'

'Open it!'

Slowly Japhet raised the lid of his case; the conductor was down on him in a flash.

'I thought so! Fireworks!'

'It was only a bit of one,' Japhet said, 'but perhaps more came out than I meant. And I didn't light it. I'm sorry, though.'

'You'll be sorry. You ought to have your brains tested, the pair of you, except there wouldn't be nothing to test. Endangering life and limb – you ought to be had up. I shall report this. What school?'

Japhet told him. 'Bad luck any school with you in it,'

said the conductor, writing down the name, also their names and addresses. 'No decent lunatic asylum'd take you!'

'I expect they can be mended,' said David, fitting the pieces of his glasses together. He was still rather dazed. Some of the other passengers were starting to murmur restlessly about being late or missing their trains.

'Think yourselves lucky you're here to *be* late!' the conductor told them irritably. 'With a pair of raving idiots like this on board, you might have been blown to kingdom come. Go on, you two, hop it. Clear out.'

'But—'

'D'you mean get off?'

'What I said and what I mean, and right quick about it.'

'But we'll be late for school.'

'It's another mile – more!'

'Then you can foot it, can't you?'

'But we've got our seasons.'

'I wouldn't care if you was life members, I'm not starting this bus till you're off.' Now the passengers were grumbling even more, so Japhet and Podge had to push towards the door between hostile and disapproving faces.

'These youngsters nowadays. . . .'

'Time they brought back the birch. . . .'

'It's all this telly. . . .'

'No business to be able to buy them things at all. . . .'

'Might have blinded him for life. . . .'

'What they're coming to today, I don't know, I'm sure. . . .'

From these and other such sickening remarks Podge and Japhet were only too glad to escape. They jumped down into the wet ditch; the bus moved on.

It had started to rain.

'We could hitch,' said Podge.

'We'll be late as it is.'

'What are we going to say?'

'Just that the bus broke down.'

'That's no good; Lena Marsh was on it, in the front. She'll go and tell.'

Lena Marsh was a pale girl with a face like a good, anxious rat; she was Miss McCormick's pet, and always came second in class after Nigel Netherwell. Certainly you couldn't trust Lena Marsh.

'There'll be an awful row,' said Podge morosely. 'And it's scripture today too.' He stood with the fine rain powdering his jacket, a picture of dejection.

'I know!' said Japhet, 'let's not go!'

'What, not at all?'

'We could hitch into Gosbridge. Go to Woolworth's. I've got sixpence halfpenny – and my lunch.'

'What? Meat?'

'No, but you can get ham rolls in Woolworth's. Anyway, it's hardly worth going to school now. Miss prayers. Not be there when she gives out the books.

Perhaps get in halfway through geography. It's not worth it.'

'What about tomorrow, then?' But Japhet had worked himself up to a state of determination; besides, for him tomorrow was always a very long way off.

'Oh, we'll think of something tomorrow. We can write notes for ourselves saying we're suddenly taken ill.'

'But Lena Marsh—'

'It's only her word against our parents'.'

'You mean *forge* notes?'

'Well, it's only this once. My mother might even actually write one, if I look ill enough,' Japhet added. The idea of forgery was perhaps a bit much.

'You don't,' said Podge.

'I shall, if we stand here in the rain much longer.'

'My Mum's never writ a note all the time I been there,' said Podge. 'It'd look funny. Besides, she hasn't got no paper, only picture post-cards, which'd be a waste. . . .'

But Japhet wasn't listening: he had hailed a passing lorry. It was called 'Pinks Ladders'. To his surprise – and very slightly to his alarm – it pulled up at once. Out of the driving-seat leaned a man with a perfectly bald head and a huge grey handle-bar moustache. Yes, he was going Gosbridge way. If they jumped in, and didn't mind the squash, and kept their feet out of his dinner-box and their heads tucked under the ladders, well, all right.

They climbed in; the bright new yellow ladders did stick into the backs of their necks, but who cared? This is life, thought Japhet.

'What d'you have for your dinner?' asked Podge.

So they started talking, and the lorry bowled along the wet road.

'Fork right for Gosbridge,' said Japhet.

'I know,' said the man, and forked left.

Japhet looked at Podge and shrugged. He supposed it was another way round. The lorry gathered speed, dashing through puddles.

'This is good,' said Podge, who had begun to catch on to the spirit of the thing. Japhet settled down to examine the dashboard and move with the jolts and enjoy himself, not thinking about tomorrow.

Louisa, at the same time, was thinking of almost nothing else. For tomorrow was Speech Day; and today the rehearsal.

Everything at her school was always most painstakingly rehearsed; by the time a play was ready, even the scene-shifters knew all the parts; concerts were rehearsed until everyone was telling everyone else for goodness sake to stop humming the pieces; the choir was not considered to have practised properly until thirty-six mouths opened as one. Now, they even had a stand-in for the bishop who was to give away the prizes. Miss Fletcher, the second mistress, held an old biology book and pretended to give it to each girl in turn; they had to take it, shake hands and smile, in that order. Lucy Baxendale had to do it again because she smiled too soon; Alice Good shook hands with the wrong hand and dropped the book; it all took a long time.

'And if he says something to you,' said Miss Fletcher, 'don't just walk away. Try to look intelligent. If you answer, speak up, don't mutter. And remember, I want to see clean blouses, tidy hair and straight ties.'

'What on earth are you doing?' Louisa's friend Georgia asked her in the cloakroom. Louisa was peering intently into the mirror.

'Trying to look intelligent.'

'Well, don't, it might put the bishop off.'

'Things don't put bishops off.'

'It'll make me giggle, then.'

'You would anyway, you always do.'

'Well, if you had to sit opposite Kathleen Pipp playing the recorder – honestly, her face!'

'Don't look at it.'

'I can't help it, it's so like a moon, specially when she blows a high note.'

'For goodness sake don't giggle in *Greensleeves*, or you'll make a squeak.'

'Oh dear,' sighed Georgia, 'I wish tomorrow was over.'

'I want tomorrow to be quick,' said Rose to Oats, 'because I'm going back to school to tell them about our accident; besides, my comic comes.'

'And tomorrow,' said Edith Slater, 'he's going for his first proper walk. I do hope it's fine.' Oats gave his one-sided smile.

A hope, a dread, a blank – how different tomorrow is for different people. The only thing that makes it the same is that what it may bring is still quite unknown; even more unknown than the road on which Japhet and Podge were now travelling at sixty miles an hour in the blinding rain.

Chapter Eight

'JUST because you both had a shock,' said Louisa, 'doesn't mean he's your dog.'

'I never said he was, Rose retorted, 'he only thinks he is. I can't help what he thinks, can I?'

'*Do* they think?' their mother asked vaguely as she blew out a toasted bun that had caught alight.

'I don't want that one,' began Rose, but Edith Slater assured them that she much preferred burnt buns, and that of course dogs thought, otherwise how could they dream?

'Japhet's late,' said their mother.

'You shouldn't feed him at table,' Louisa told Rose, who was making Oats beg for her crusts.

'I'm not,' said Rose. 'This is not feeding.' Such quibbles infuriated Louisa.

'Honestly, she never admits anything. She's got no idea of the truth. Wait till you do science, you'll be in a nice mess: mixing up all the wrong things and then saying you weren't.'

'Oh do stop arguing,' said their mother, 'and Rose, make Oats get down; I will not have his chin on the cake. I suppose I'll have to keep these buns hot – I wonder if he's missed the bus.'

The four of them sat in the kitchen having tea; outside, the sky was broken and stormy; the last of the roses had been blowing in the rain all day, and people were saying winter had come.

Oats put his chin on Rose's knee.

'Perhaps we've got a little bit of electricity left in us,' she said, 'and he can smell it.'

Louisa told her not to be ridiculous; nevertheless, there did seem to be some new and special attachment between Rose and Oats. Everywhere she went, he went too; he had lain in her bedroom for two whole days, making hairs all over the carpet and licking up the biscuit crumbs or bits of potato crisp she had dropped on the floor; he even sat and waited for her outside the bathroom.

'Just a moment, Oats,' she would call patiently and clearly when he whined. And when she came out he would lick her and jump up as if they hadn't met for weeks. It was really rather strange; all the same, Louisa wasn't going to have Oats being Rose's dog.

'You've got your rabbit,' she said, 'which you never feed.'

'Oh I do!'

'I did them all this morning, and yesterday.'

'Last Sunday—' began Rose indignantly, but their mother put a stop to this new argument. Besides, the rabbits were a touchy subject with Edith Slater, who thought it was cruel to keep them at all, sitting in their hutches just waiting for food all day long; if she had her way, they would all be allowed to run wild. Japhet had assured her that they'd only be killed by other, wilder rabbits, or by foxes, or by Stephen Carter with his airgun. Stephen lived half a mile up the road and went to boarding-school, but sometimes he was at home for week-ends, and then the woods broke with an occasional shot. Rose would say, 'Some poor pigeon,' and they would all feel uncomfortable; perhaps it was because they had not lived in the country all their lives.

'Where are the buttons?' asked Louisa. 'There's been one off my blouse for about a month.' The demands of Speech Day were weighing on her; she wondered if she ought to wash her hair.

'The button-box is missing,' their mother said, 'you'd better look in the vase.'

It wasn't until Louisa had turned out the vase and all the other small flower-jugs, bowls and mugs in the house that Rose said dreamily, '*I* know where there's a button.' And she and Oats fetched it from the dolls' house. 'It was their plate,' she said, 'but never mind.'

'Plates don't have holes,' said Louisa, 'and you might have told me before.'

'A plate for ornament,' said Rose; 'they're on a diet.'

Louisa was exasperated; what with Rose, and this house where nothing was ever in the right place, and the kitchen table where tea always seemed to be half-finished and homework half-begun. . . . Compare it with Georgia's house, she thought; all oak panelling and chromium ash-trays and a special television-room: yes, but she never really felt comfortable there. On the other hand, compare it with the mushroom man's – Mr Browne's – that pinched, quiet cottage, and that boy there working all alone as the autumn evenings drew in. Louisa looked at the ragged sky outside, and the cluttered kitchen, with its bright light, the ironing-board up, buns under the grill, Rose's comic nearly in the jam, conkers all over the top of the fridge. She sighed contentedly and sewed on her button.

'Where *is* that boy?' their mother fretted. 'The second bus has gone now – what on earth can he be up to?'

But no one paid much attention. Rose and Oats were looking at TV; Edith was grating cheese; Louisa just said in a detached voice, 'Perhaps he walked,' and went on eating, between stitches, the gratings that came her way.

'He's never been as late as this before,' said their mother. 'It'll be dark soon. And he didn't take his mac.'

'Don't worry,' said Louisa, 'he'll turn up. He always does.'

'I should hope so,' said their mother. Edith Slater

merely sighed, 'Boys!' which might have meant anything; or it could have been that she had just grated her knuckles.

If only they had known – but perhaps it was just as well. Certainly none of them would have guessed, in their wildest dreams, where Japhet was at that moment – or even what he looked like.

We must skid back to the wet road of the morning. And the lorry gathering speed; and the bald-headed man humming *Somewhere Over the Rainbow* through his huge moustache.

'I say,' said Japhet, 'this is not the way to Gosbridge.'

'I'll 'ave three guesses,' said the man as if Japhet had not spoken. 'First, you bunked school.' He glanced sideways at Podge, who grinned sheepishly.

'See? Right. Second, you wanted a bit of a lark.'

'We just thought of going to Woolworth's,' said Japhet, 'that's all.'

'No reason why you shouldn't,' said the man, 'no reason at all. There's Woolworths everywhere.' He took a bend at speed; water splashed up all over Podge, who was sitting on the outside.

'And third guess lucky, which is *why* you wanted a lark this particular a.m. Which is, to put it bluntly, you was in a spot of trouble. Right?'

Podge looked at Japhet, who hesitated. But the man waved him aside.

'No need to say; no need at all. I'm not prying; you don't have to tell me. All I says to myself is, I says, here's two blokes in trouble: well, you wouldn't be standing in a damp ditch first thing of a rainy morning for the sheer joy of it, would you now?'

'No,' said Japhet, 'we weren't. But where are we going? This is *not* the way to—'

'Listen,' said the man, 'don't you worry. You want to go to Gosbridge, I'm taking you to Gosbridge. Only we might have to go a bit of a way round, that's all. O.K. for a lark?'

'How much round?'

'Oh, just there and back.'

'Sure about back?' Podge was anxious; partly because that ham roll was growing dim, partly because he was so wet all down one side.

'Course I'm sure about back. Wherever I go, I always come back. Well, I wouldn't be 'ere now if I didn't, would I? New York, I've been: and back. Singapore: and back. Tokyo, Cape Town, Melbourne, Rangoon – more places than what I can remember: and always back. That's the art of it, see.'

'The art of what?' Japhet asked.

'I call it the art of livin',' said the man, negotiating what could have been a deadly skid. 'But perhaps that's a bit deep for you. What I mean is, people nowadays, they don't know 'ow to live. No adventure. It's all sittin' at home and let the telly do it for you. Now I've always

74

believed in being as I term it mobile. Provided, of course – as your pal here very rightly points out – provided you get back. Which I guarantee you will.'

Japhet stared at the double curve of the windscreen-wipers as they sliced across the streaming glass. He was beginning to wonder if this man were mad. His driving certainly suggested it, let alone his talk. But what could they do? They were going much too fast to jump out; no other cars would see or hear them, through the rain, if they shouted or waved; and to try to snatch at the brakes would be certain disaster. Japhet glanced at Podge, and saw that he was rather white. But this made Japhet pull himself together; after all, it was his idea to be in the lorry at all; it was up to him to make the best of it. Besides, if the man were mad, it seemed quite a nice kind of madness: for instance, he was very sympathetic when they told him about Miss McCormick; he even said that for his part, he didn't hold with school at all. He had run away from it when he was twelve. This put Podge on his side at once. As for Japhet, he decided that there was nothing to be done but to meet adventure as it came, and enjoy it. He was ready for anything.

But not quite ready for what came next.

'All right,' he said cheerfully, 'where *are* we going?'

'Birmingham,' said the man.

A stunned silence. The man began to whistle *Over*

the Rainbow between his teeth; it sounded like a draught blown through wool.

'But that's – that's more than a hundred miles!'

'One hundred and twenty-five on the clock. I did it last week. There and back in under the seven hours.'

'I might not be home for tea,' said Podge slowly.

'Don't worry, we'll stop. I know all the places from 'ere to John o' Groats. Mind you, they're not a patch on them drive-ins they 'ave in the States. Serve you with trays straight into the car, hamburgers, apple-pie, steak, what you fancy. I'll be back there one of these days.'

'But we can't go to Birmingham,' said Japhet, feeling dazed. Gosbridge was three miles away; the difference between six and two hundred and fifty was more than he could swallow.

'Why not?' Podge and Japhet looked at each other and didn't answer.

'Well, why not? I've told you, I'll get you back. Take you into Gosbridge if you still want to. What's wrong with Birmingham?'

'I don't know; I've never been there.'

'All right, time you did. It's what I say: people are too much stick-in-the-muds. What's the point of bunking school and then just mooning round the neighbourhood? You want to get out and about a bit, see life.'

Podge still looked blank, but Japhet thought that all

this was really quite sensible; and as long as they did get back – well, as the man said, why not? Missing school at Birmingham wasn't any worse than missing it just round the corner; and tomorrow was a long way off.

'How did you manage to go to all those places?' he asked. They were now on a straight road, doing a steady sixty-five; the ladders bounced, the doors rattled.

'Cuttin' hair,' said the man. Japhet glanced at his bald head.

'All right, you can laugh. They all chip me about it, but I don't worry, I can fall back on my moustache.'

'D'you mean you're really a barber?'

'That's right. I'm only doin' this for the time being, to oblige a friend. Cuttin' hair's my job. Yes, I've been all over the world, cuttin' hair,' he went on ruminatively. 'Ships, you see. Get a job on a ship – work your passage – never mind where to – and there you are. Well, they all want their hair cut, time to time. Then I settle down for a bit or I might get another ship back, all accordin'.'

Japhet was very much interested; this was a career he hadn't thought of, and it sounded like an easy way of seeing life. All you needed was a comb and scissors, and no Eleven Plus. Podge wasn't so much impressed.

'What's the food like?' he asked.

'On the ships, good. When you get there – well, that depends. There's not much I haven't eaten, by and

77

large. Birds' nest soup; frogs; fried blubber, baked coconuts – well, I'm still 'ere, aren't I?'

'I'll stick to sausages,' said Podge.

The man then told them that he still did cut hair, even while he drove this lorry. He carried his scissors and things with him, and would always give a short back and sides to any of the other drivers in the roadside pull-ups, in return for a cup of tea and a wad.

'What's a wad?'

'See what I mean? Call it schoolin', and they don't teach you a simple thing like that. Come on, I'll show you.'

And he pulled up suddenly by a shack labelled 'Café'; so suddenly that Podge and Japhet fell forward and bumped their heads hard against the windscreen.

'You want to sit back more,' said the man placidly as they stumbled across the mud where several other lorries were parked.

Still rather dazed, they went into the steamy café and were given a choice of bath buns, sticky buns or things with coconut whiskers.

'They're all wads,' said the man, 'so fill up.'

Podge had one of each; Japhet chose the sticky buns and wiped his hands on the insides of his pockets. They all had strong sweet tea.

'Come to look at you,' said the man, sipping thoughtfully, 'you could do with a bit of a tidy up, the pair of you. Not to say styling.'

'I had mine cut Saturday,' said Podge defensively.

'You never! 'Ow much did he charge?'

'Two bob.'

'It's daylight robbery. Well, look at that tuft: just look at it!' Podge, of course, couldn't, and Japhet had always taken it for granted. 'Two bob, and leave a thing like that! 'Ere, I'll do you for nothing. I can't sit and see a job left in that state, it's an insult to the profession.'

And before they knew where they were, he had whipped out a grimy whitish cloth which he draped round Podge's neck, and a pair of scissors with which he attacked Podge's thick mole-coloured hair.

'Come on,' he said to Japhet, 'your turn.'

'I thought we were going to Birmingham.'

'Plenty of time. Sit still.'

They did get to Birmingham – but only to the outskirts, for a quarter of an hour, while the man delivered the ladders. It was still raining finely and, by the time they had had another wad, they all thought they had better make for home. Japhet was secretly disappointed: his chief impressions were of dampness, dinginess, red brick and advertisement hoardings. Still, the ride was good: on the way back, the man drove even faster because the lorry was empty; they clung to their seats and expected to be overturned at any moment. Japhet began to feel sick, but wouldn't have admitted it for the world.

'Smashing!' he said faintly as the man slowed down at last to drop him outside his own house.

It was after six, and quite dark. They had been out for nearly ten hours.

Japhet's courage began to evaporate as he walked to the back door. The time; and missing school. . . . And then, to his dismay, he saw that Tilley lamp standing under the porch; the mushroom man could only have come about the firework. To make matters worse, he knew his mother hated very short hair; and 'Pinks Ladders' had said proudly that his would probably be the shortest crew-cut in the world.

Chapter Nine

'You could have gone and picked it up,' said Louisa.

'What, in front of the bishop?'

'He wouldn't have minded. Well, less than listening to *Greensleeves* with Kathleen Pipp playing the bottom, and no top. It's not as if recorders don't sound funny anyway.'

'I couldn't help it,' Georgia protested. 'Jane Briggs was supposed to be top too, but when she saw I'd dropped it she just stopped, silly ass. Besides,' she added, 'it rolled right into the hydrangeas.'

'Oh well, never mind. Perhaps he thought Kathleen Pipp was supposed to be a solo.'

'It's all her fault,' said Georgia, 'she shouldn't *look* like that. I told you she put me off.'

'People can't help what they look like.'

'My mother says they jolly well can. She says that any woman can be beautiful if she sets her mind to it.'

'But some people's minds are so queer to start with,'

said Louisa. 'I suppose Kathleen Pipp might be all right,' she added doubtfully, 'in about ten years. But she might not. Not everybody is.'

'My mother says you only have to decide on your type.'

Georgia looked hopefully into the cloakroom mirror; Louisa sat on a bench with her head against her shoe-bag and thought of Georgia's mother, who always seemed to her to be all type and no person. She had once seen the dressing-table there; it was laid out with pots and jars and brushes and a battalion of lipsticks; her own mother kept a bottle of nail-varnish in the kitchen medicine cupboard, with nameless dog-pills, and a worn-down lipstick refill at the bottom of her handbag with the last of the shells they had collected in the summer holidays. These shells always stayed there until next year; in Georgia's house they would have been placed in a crystal bowl of water and put on the huge television set with the silver golf cups. Georgia's mother was like that too, thought Louisa; everything perfect and in place; everything to match; everything so polished and filed and smooth that you wondered how she could ever do anything ordinary such as go to bed or make a piece of toast. And how she could have had a daughter like Georgia, all giggles and black greasy hair that wouldn't stay in a pony-tail for five minutes without the sides coming down, even when she stuck them up with soap.

'Anyway, thank goodness she didn't come,' said Georgia; 'I knew she wouldn't, it was the Bridge Club tea.'

Louisa reflected that she would rather her own mother were there, even to see her drop a recorder; but Georgia seemed quite happy, so perhaps there was no need to be sorry. Even being an only child brought its advantages: Georgia had magnificent Christmas presents such as a pony or a tennis court – and no brothers or sisters to make trouble. And thinking of trouble, and hoping to take Georgia's mind off the recorder, Louisa began to tell about Japhet. Georgia 'Goshed' and 'Oh-Lummied' in all the right places; Louisa herself was secretly proud of having a brother who could do so many awful things in one day.

'The funny part was,' she said, 'about the cap. At first we thought the mushroom man – Mr Browne – was going to raise the roof about the glasses, or what might have happened to David's eyes, but all he was worried about was the cap. He said the other was on the National Health, but the cap cost six-and-eleven.'

'Why didn't you give it to him?' Of course six-and-eleven to Georgia was about twopence to an ordinary person; but even so, Louisa had to try to explain that you couldn't offer money to somebody like Mr Browne. She remembered his proud, offended refusal of that ten-shilling note; now, as then, it was a question of the right thing or nothing at all.

'That cap just has to be found,' she said, 'or we shall feel terrible for ever. Only there are so many blackberry bushes.'

'Hey!' said Georgia. 'I just remembered, I'm supposed to be helping clear up the marquee!'

'You really are the limit, it'll be done by now.'

'Oh dear, I shan't get a tick. Come with me?' Georgia looked agitated; she relied upon Louisa very much, and Louisa often felt older and wiser, in spite of Georgia's being nearly fifteen, and having all that oak panelling at home, and cocktail parties where she handed round strange food.

They went together to the darkening marquee that had been put up for the bishop's and the parents' tea; a few wafer-thin sandwiches curled separately on plates in corners of the grass; an abandoned umbrella stood against the last trestle table; the school matron, with a list clamped to a board, was looking absent-mindedly tense.

'Ah, Georgia! At last! This table – why weren't you here before? Louisa, I haven't got you down. Where are those Fifth Form people – I ticked them all and now they're not here, really it's too bad. . . .'

'Never mind, Matron, we'll manage,' said Louisa comfortingly; in a few minutes the trestle table was dismantled and Georgia had her tick. Ticks, you will have realized, were very important in this school; there were occasions when you were liable to be counted as not there at all unless you had one, even when you had been there all the time.

The marquee was nearly dark. 'It's rather horrid, isn't it,' said Louisa, 'when everything's over?'

'This fish paste's disgusting.' Georgia threw away the remains of the last sandwich and heeled it into the grass.

'And all those Old Girls,' Louisa went on, 'coming up for their prizes in ordinary clothes – doesn't it make you sort of turn over inside? Only three more Speech Days and we may be like them.'

'Gosh, I'd never trot across the platform with a huge white handbag like Sonia Blogg. Or dye my hair that yellow. And did you see Anthea's skirt? Honestly! Still, I shall never have to go up for a prize anyway, so it doesn't matter.'

'You might.' But Louisa knew that Georgia probably wouldn't; and that she would certainly never understand this melancholy end-of-the-year feeling that came as you scuffed your feet through the fallen leaves in the dusk, and saw single lights in red-brick buildings, and heard a boarder practising arpeggios far away.

But Louisa was not the kind of person to feel melancholy for long without asking the reason why, and doing something about it.

'I know your mother didn't come,' she said, 'but

wouldn't it be awful not to have a mother *not* to come?'

Georgia supposed it would.

'Everybody ought to have a mother,' said Louisa firmly.

Georgia supposed they ought.

'It's peculiar, a kitchen without a woman in it.'

Georgia supposed it was, though the woman in her kitchen was a fat Hungarian cook who didn't speak a word of English, except 'Omelets tonight?'

'The point is,' said Louisa as they came back to the cloakroom, 'how do you find somebody a nice wife? Well, any wife?'

'It depends who. Most people find their own. Why?'

'Oh, I was just thinking. I mean, for instance, it's awful, Japhet having his hair cut short like that, but it would be much worse if there was nobody to mind. Fathers don't mind much about that sort of thing – they think more about caps costing six-and-eleven.'

'I don't know what you're talking about,' said Georgia. So Louisa told her about the mushroom man, and the boy, and the cottage – realizing, as she told, that this was the picture that always came to her when she felt at all depressed, or it was evening, or things were over. The bishop had talked to them invigoratingly that afternoon about Charity, and Service, and Living for Others; but all these seemed vague words, mere clouds round the single sharp figure of that boy in the apron and that man with the Tilley lamp and no smile. The more Louisa thought of them, the more she felt haunted: and when Georgia said, 'Oh well, let's think about Christmas,' it was even worse. What would that man and that boy do in the cottage, having Christmas all alone? Would they solemnly pull two red crackers? No: Mr Browne had said the very word 'Christmas' as if it hurt him to think about it. He certainly wouldn't spend money on frivolous things like crackers. Perhaps a chicken, or a very small turkey? And one or two paper chains: the kind you bought in packets and gummed and linked together? Louisa could see them, hanging skinnily across that naked light. And David almost certainly wouldn't hang up a stocking; impossible to imagine Mr Browne creeping upstairs at midnight with rustlings and thuds of apples: and he would surely never decorate a tree. . . .

'I do wish they could find somebody,' she said to Georgia. 'It wouldn't matter what she looked like – much; just somebody homely and comfortable, to be there when they came in.'

'There are Marriage Bureaux,' said Georgia, 'where you can put your name down on a list. A friend of my mother's runs one; I think they're horrid.'

'So do I,' said Louisa, who had actually never heard of such things until now. 'Still, I could make a list – I mean, of all the people who might do.'

'What, and send it to him?'

'Don't be soft; first I should sort them out into likelies and unlikelies; then I should go and see them and try to find out if they had anyone else in mind; then – well, then I suppose I should have to arrange some sort of meeting.'

'I think you're batty,' said Georgia; and Louisa, catching sight of her own round face in the cloakroom mirror, grinned and agreed. But that didn't stop her from being haunted; besides, she loved making lists.

As for Japhet – here we might quote from the book Louisa had for her form prize. It was by Jane Austen, who landed her characters in a really terrible mess and then began a chapter: 'Let other pens dwell on guilt and misery. I quit such odious subjects as quickly as possible. . . .' And then she polished them off very quickly indeed, each to his or her most suitable fate. We feel a little like this about Japhet – except for the polishing off; and also for the fact that although he did feel guilty, he could never be miserable for very long. And his hair would grow. But the trouble he was in for the moment, on all sides, hardly bears repeating; we think that for Japhet's sake we ought to slide over it lightly. Or, as he would have said, 'For Pete's sake!'

'*Not* Pete's sake,' his mother would insist.

'Why not?'

'It's not a nice expression.'

'What's wrong with Pete?'

'Pete who?' (Rose, off the point as usual.)

'Oh golly, can I have some milk?'

'*Not* golly. . . .' And so it would go on. We need only note that Japhet had come home to find his father furious, his mother shocked, the mushroom man grim, Louisa and Rose disapproving: only Oats and Edith Slater took his side at all, Oats by definite licks, Edith more vaguely.

'I went to Birmingham once,' she said, 'and fed the sparrows in some square. They were so tame; I'll never forget the little Black Country sparrows.'

As for Miss McCormick: but as you know, she could be very nasty indeed, and Japhet would hate us to repeat the things she said to him. The final touch was her keeping up the pretence of not recognizing him because of his hair; this made the others feebly laugh, which was the worst of all. Old Mr Glynn actually *didn't* recognize Japhet, and said several times, peering kindly, 'Ah, a new boy! Never mind, I dare say you'll catch up.'

Podge was in the same amount of trouble at school, but less at home. His Mum merely said, 'Wherever've you bin? The chips are all gone soft'; and when Podge muttered, 'Birmingham,' she told him not to give her those tales. His Dad was angry about having the tea-things on so late; but he was always fairly angry anyway. He gave Podge the usual whack over the ear, after which Podge settled down to the soft chips and heard no more about it.

Japhet's father, on the other hand, never whacked people, but he decided that this time Japhet really must do some sort of penance. So he set him to chop a huge pile of wood in the chicken-house: a job Japhet hated, because it took the whole of Saturday morning and gave him splinters.

'Couldn't I mix that sand and cement you've got instead?'

'No.'

'Couldn't I dig the garden?'

'No.'

'Or weed?'

'No.'

'It does need weeding—' Japhet began desperately.

'I know. Go and chop the wood.'

And this on the Saturday morning when it seemed a particularly good idea to take Oats across the field and light a fire. But you never know how things will turn out. For if his father hadn't been so firm, Japhet would never have come tearing indoors two minutes later, with his pinkest face and his topmost squeak:

'Come and see what's in the chicken-house! Come quickly!'

Chapter Ten

THE THREE kittens sat on a cement-sack; one tabby, one black and white, and one all colours, mottled.

'That poor cat of Mrs Tucker's,' said Louisa. 'It probably had them out in the field. It has them anywhere.'

'Aren't they absolutely sweet,' said Rose.

'Don't touch them, they'll be frightened,' Japhet told her, picking one up neatly by the scruff of its neck. He put it back; the kittens mewed, one after the other, as if they had learned not to talk all at once.

'Here comes the mother,' Louisa said, 'looking for them.' Mrs Tucker's bedraggled cat, patched with tabby and ginger and black and white, slunk round the chicken-house door. The kittens jumped off the sack and ran to her, this time mewing all together.

'I'm going to fetch them some milk,' said Japhet. He came back with a saucer; most of the milk had slopped off by the time he put it down.

'Did you warm it?' Louisa asked. 'They can't have it straight out of the fridge.'

She went indoors and came back with the jug of left-over coffee-milk from breakfast and three saucers. By this time Rose and Japhet were each holding a kitten. The third – the black and white one – had hidden under the wood pile.

'Now you'll have to move all that,' said Louisa, 'to get him out.'

'How can I, I'm holding this?'

'Nor can I,' said Rose, and clutched the tabby kitten tighter.

'Don't, you'll hurt it,' Japhet said. 'Why don't you hold it like I do?'

Louisa noticed, as she often had, that Japhet was really very good at handling animals; kind and firm and natural. His kitten was purring already; Rose's mewed and struggled. Louisa went on moving huge lengths of wood from the back of the pile; she became covered with shreds of rotted bark and had three splinters and a bruised toe; then the black and white kitten ran out of the front of the wood by itself. She picked it up and hugged it; bruises and splinters didn't matter.

'Can we keep one?' asked Rose.

'Let's go and ask Mrs Tucker.'

Louisa reminded Japhet that it was more important to ask their mother and father, who had said No to cats ever since their last one was run over. But that was in London, years ago. 'We can try,' she said.

So they went into the kitchen, where Edith Slater was giving Oats his elevenses – all the broken bits out of the biscuit-tin.

'If there aren't enough,' she said, 'we allow ourselves a little shake, don't we, old boy?' Oats smiled as usual while she put the lid on the tin and shook vigorously.

'There! The digestives always break up beautifully,' she said with triumph. Louisa had once objected that you might just as well take a whole biscuit to start with; Edith had stared at her in amazement and said, 'But he's only *allowed* to have the broken ones.' So every day she shook the tin.

Edith said the kittens were darlings, and that she should think they were about five or six weeks old, and that it was really cruel to take them away from their mother at all, but that she hoped and prayed they would find good homes.

'This is a good home,' said Japhet, and went to find his father in the study. Oats was highly excited about the kittens, in a friendly way; he only wanted to see them and have a sniff, but each kitten spat at him so hard that he retired, surprised.

At first their father said No.

'Oh please!' they all pleaded. Still No.

'You don't even look after the rabbits,' he said.

'It'll be me who has to see to it,' their mother said

with more feeling than grammar. They assured her she wouldn't; Japhet begged, Louisa promised, Rose cried. No. They all made most earnest vows about the rabbits; never again would their father have to hose them out on Sunday afternoon; never again would they forget the oats; they would truly and always and faithfully look after the rabbits. No, no.

'But look, he's such a dear little thing,' said Japhet, putting his kitten down on the desk. The others did the same; three kittens walked round the blotting-pad, mewing. Their father picked one up; it immediately started to purr. Louisa repeated that they would honestly turn over a new leaf with the rabbits; their father's kitten purred more loudly.

'Well . . .' he said, and looked at their mother.

'Well . . .' she sighed.

'Yipee!' said Japhet.

'Now wait a minute, nobody said anything about—' But everyone knew the argument was over. The only thing that remained was to decide which kitten to keep.

'Mine!' said Rose.

'Mine!'

'Mine!'

'Can't we keep them all?' This time, both their parents said No so firmly that there was no point in going on.

'Look, mine's a lovely little one,' Japhet said, 'it's

got an orange ear.'

'Have the tabby,' Rose begged, squeezing it.

'This one,' said Louisa, 'has much the most character. It pretended to be stuck under the wood-pile when it wasn't.'

They began to argue, until their father said the only thing was to draw lots.

'Heads or tails,' said Japhet.

'There are three,' Louisa pointed out. Their father was tearing up strips of paper; one of these he marked with a cross.

'The person who draws the cross can choose.' He screwed up the papers and muddled them. They stood round with their kittens and watched; no one had even noticed that they were all wearing their wellington boots in the house.

Rose uncrumpled a plain paper.

Louisa uncrumpled a plain paper.

So did Japhet. Their father drew one himself; it was plain. Their mother took the last paper, with the cross.

'Well, I don't like such piebald cats as that,' she said, looking at Japhet's. 'I think it might grow up to be an alley cat.'

'We haven't got an alley,' said Japhet.

'Still, it might. And we had a tabby before, and it was run over, perhaps because they're harder to see in the dark—'

'So it's this one!' Louisa took the black and white kitten to meet Oats; Japhet and Rose went sadly but resignedly back to Mrs Tucker with the others. Edith Slater sent messages about egg yolk and the R.S.P.C.A., but Mrs Tucker was too deaf to hear.

The next thing was to think of a name. They sat at lunch making suggestions.

'Tiny Tim,' said Japhet, who had just read *A Christmas Carol*, and liked it in spite of the fact that it was on Miss McCormick's list.

'What when he's *not* tiny?' said Rose.

'Bingo,' their father murmured.

'That's a dog's name.'

Rose suggested Cinderella. 'Why?' asked Louisa; Rose didn't know.

'Muffin,' said their mother.

'Crumpet,' their father added.

'I think in the Midlands they call them pikelets,' said Edith Slater dreamily.

Louisa brought them back to earth. 'Imagine calling a kitten Pikelet!' she said. 'Outside at night, Pikelet, Pikelet, Pikelet! Anyway, we don't know if it's a boy or a girl, so we shall have to choose a neutral name.'

'What's neutral?' asked Rose.

'Either. Like – well, Spot, or Smudge, or Fluffy—'

'They're too usual,' Rose objected.

'Bathplug,' said Japhet, and started to laugh; then they all suggested sillier and sillier names – you can imagine the sort – too silly to write down. At last Louisa said firmly that they ought to make a list. She took a pencil from the fruit-bowl and an old envelope out of a cookery book, and wrote down all the sensible suggestions so far.

In the end the kitten was called none of these; its name was Winter.

'But this is only autumn,' Rose complained.

'White snow, black coal,' said Louisa; 'I think Winter's a good name.' And they were all tired of arguing, and there was still the washing-up to do; so Winter was put in the play-room with a tray of earth.

Just a word about this play-room, because it has an important part in the story. It had been a kitchen when the house was two cottages; there was still a brick floor there, and a place where the sink had been, though this was now concealed by the old upright piano that had come from their great-grandfather and was over seventy years old. The piano had garlands of inlaid wood, and marks where brass candlesticks had been removed; Louisa practised on it before breakfast every day. Rose practised on the night before her music lesson. The play-room also had a back door – once the main door of the second cottage. This door now led to nothing, but opened almost against Mrs Tucker's hedge; there was a narrow strip of rough grass between the hedge and the side of their house. The strip sloped up past the chicken-house towards the field; not a slope you would notice unless, for instance – but we mustn't jump ahead.

This was the Saturday when their parents were going out. So of course it started to rain. 'Just when I've set my hair,' their mother sighed. And tea had to be early, because she must leave the supper ready; she washed-up the plates as they used them.

'Can't I even have more *bread*?' Japhet asked indignantly as his plate was whipped away. His mother gave him the board and the remains of a cut loaf; he made himself a pile of Marmite sandwiches and took them in to watch TV. Rose was already installed there with Oats; Japhet fetched Winter from the play-room, set him on his shoulder and settled down.

By now it was raining hard; their mother said it always did when she was going out. She began to prepare the supper-trays, giving Edith Slater instructions as to which was which.

'The jelly and the banana's Japhet's; the jelly and cut-up pear for Rose – I hope the pear won't be too brown. Japhet the sandwiches, Rose the Ryvita—'

'*More* sandwiches?' said Edith, surprised. 'Do you think he gets enough protein?'

'No,' sighed their mother. Louisa reassured her about all that milk.

'Oh and there are some grapes: a few on top of each, only do deal them out, there must be the same number on each.'

'Are they washed?' Louisa asked without looking up. She was sitting at the kitchen table making a list. Her mother washed the grapes.

'There's the cold meat for you and Edith.'

'What time do they have to go to bed?' Louisa regarded herself as one of the grown-ups on occasions like this.

'Whose bath is it?' her mother said.

'I'll go and look at the rota.' Louisa came back with the news that it was Japhet's bath, and that Rose had forgotten to underline her name last night. The bath rota had been Louisa's idea; it was a large piece of cardboard that hung on a pink tape on a hook in the bathroom, with a pencil attached. Louisa had made out a list of baths for the next four months; a note at the bottom said, 'Please underline your name when you have had your bath. Even if you miss your bath, underline your name to avoid confusion.' The way people mistook the date, or forgot to underline, or took away the pencil, or left it broken, caused Louisa much despair: but on nights such as this, the rota came into its own.

Bedtimes were decided by TV programmes. Rose was to go to bed at eight; but Louisa said 'Underhill Trail' went on till ten past, so that was Rose's time. Japhet generally stayed up another half hour, but there was a variety show until five to nine.

'Well, he *must* go then,' their mother said to Edith

99

Slater, who nodded and blinked and might have heard or might not.

'I'll see that he does,' said Louisa. 'Only don't let him look at the advertisements, that's fatal. Besides, there's a Space thing afterwards.'

'I'm never very keen on Space,' said Edith absently.

At last everything was ready; their father had the car ticking over outside; their mother was waving wet nails about and telling Rose she couldn't possibly make a toy mouse a new nose *now*.

They drove off in pelting rain.

'I think Puddy wants some milk,' said Japhet. He pronounced it as in pudding.

'Its name is Winter,' Louisa said.

'Milk, Puddy?' asked Rose.

We may as well admit now – it's bound to come out some time – that although Louisa conscientiously went on calling the kitten Winter, Japhet and Rose and finally everyone else just said Puddy. So much for good names.

'It must be warmed,' said Edith Slater. 'Blood heat.'

'How hot is blood?' Japhet asked.

'Just so that you can put your little finger in it,' Louisa said. Japhet went for a saucer, but came back with the tea-pot from his bedroom.

'I've had a wonderful idea,' he said. 'We can fill this with Puddy's milk and keep it warm by the fire.' He put the tea-pot down in the hearth; there was a beautiful coal fire instead of the usual electric one, and Rose had been promised that she could roast some chestnuts provided she had her pyjamas and dressing-gown on first.

'Just listen to the rain,' she said as Japhet went to fetch the milk.

'And some poor stray animals out in it,' sighed Edith Slater. Louisa looked into the fire; she heard the beat of the rain against the windows and the long frantic owl-calls of the wind in the chimney and round the roof; she was glad they were safe and warm.

Japhet came back and took the lid off the tea-pot. 'Oh, I forgot,' he said, 'there's something in it.'

'What?'

'Never mind. Just something of mine.' He put the lid back on. Louisa told him that if he set a cold bottle of milk by the fire it would crack. 'How batty can you get?' Exasperated, she went to warm the milk properly on the stove, even using the glass thing in the saucepan that was supposed to prevent its boiling over, but never did.

'I think Puddy wants his earth,' observed Rose. And she took the kitten to the play-room.

'I wonder if its poor mother had time to teach it to wash—' Edith was beginning, when there was a desperate shriek.

'*Now* what's the matter?' snapped Louisa, coming

back with the milk. Rose made such fusses about so little.

But not this time.

'Come quickly, quickly!' yelled Rose. 'The play-room's all wet!'

'*Wet!*' Louisa went to the door and stood aghast. 'It's floating! Japhet! Edith! Hurry!' They did.

'Good gracious me, a flood,' said Edith.

'What fool left that door open?' Japhet asked.

'It's all coming through here now,' said Rose, re-treating into the adjoining dining-room where nobody ever dined.

'It's a foot deep!' Edith said.

'It'll be two feet in a minute,' Louisa gasped, push-ing the once-back-door shut. 'Well, come on, *do* some-thing!'

'Rescue Puddy!' said Edith.

'Quick, get out the rugs,' Japhet shouted, and began to pull at one that had a table-leg caught in its hole. Even with the door shut, the water was still pouring in underneath.

'It must be coming down that slope,' said Louisa. She dashed in, freed the rug and snatched a pile of music off the stool.

'A cloudburst!' said Edith Slater, doing nothing. The water was round her feet.

'Golly, come on!' Japhet delightedly went into action. He began to drag out stools, chairs, the dolls' house, the old blackboard.

'We'd better put our boots on,' said Rose.

'Puddy's saucer!' cried Edith as a plastic dish floated towards her. 'We must save Puddy's saucer!' The water was round her ankles.

'Well, come on, help!' Japhet was hard at it, pinker every minute.

'I'm going to phone them to come back,' Louisa said, and rushed to the study. There were situations when even she felt lost without her parents.

Rose came back with wellington boots over her pyjamas. 'I couldn't find yours,' she said mournfully to Japhet.

'Oats knows where they are,' he panted, 'outside by the back porch. Never mind—' But Rose and Oats had gone to look.

'Whatever shall we do?' said Edith. 'Poor little Puddy's so frightened.' The water was round her calves.

Louisa jiggled the telephone up and down; no good. The line was out of order. Cut, she thought. Floods, storms. . . . For a moment she stood horrified. Then she decided: Fire Brigade. Go on the bicycle. Tell Japhet and Edith to use buckets, brooms, mops, anything. . . .

And in three minutes she had given Japhet instructions that he was much too pink to hear; then she rode out into the pelting dark.

103

St. HELEN'S SCHOOL
LIBRARY

The water was nearly up to Edith Slater's knees.

'Something must be done,' she said in a tone of sudden perturbed discovery. And went to place the kitten safely in Oats's basket.

Japhet was sopping wet; Rose was still outside looking for his boots.

Chapter Eleven

LOUISA RODE with her eyes screwed against the rain. It was four miles to the nearest Fire Station, in the large village where they did the Saturday shopping. Tonight the road was almost unrecognizable, swilling with water on each side and in some places right across the crest as well. When she came to the little narrow bridge where a stream ran across, there appeared to be no road at all, only a deep black pool. She got off and waded, pushing the bicycle between the brick arches of the bridge that still just showed. A car came towards her, the headlamps blinding in the wet. She ducked, and there was a great thresh of water as the car slowly passed and douched her from head to foot. She rode on.

The four miles seemed very long, but at last she arrived between the lights of the village. On one side the big grocer's with its Bacon Week display still lit up: a huge greyish plaster pig nodded its head hour after hour to the empty street, surrounded by bright eggs in trusses of straw. On the other side, the radio shop, a cave with gold and coral and sea-green illuminations where gramophones or tape recorders had been left to shine in the dark. The street was dryer here, better drained; and anyway the rain had lessened now.

The Fire Station was at the other end of the village; Louisa leaned her bicycle against a wall and rang the large brass bell. No answer. She rang again, then decided to go round to the back; no time must be lost. She had a vision of herself riding back on a fire engine that would churn through the lanes at top speed with a clanging of bells and a sizzle like violent frying as it dashed across that bridge. She hoped she might see the firemen slide down their brass rod to come into action; but perhaps that only happened in huge city Fire Stations. Anyway, she hoped the pumps would work.

There was a light in an office at the back. She knocked and went in, wet and breathless.

She expected to see a hefty fireman there, perhaps in shirt sleeves, with his helmet on the table ready. Instead, there was a woman knitting.

'I want the Fire Brigade, quickly,' said Louisa. 'We've got a flood.'

'You're not the first,' said the woman placidly, changing rows. 'They're both out on floods tonight, both engines.'

Louisa suddenly recognized her as the lady from the village wool-shop: but what on earth was she doing there?

'But we must have help, it's urgent and my parents are out and the telephone's off and the water's coming in—'

'Yes, there are a lot of lines down,' said the wool-shop lady. 'It's the storm. I haven't had a call for the last hour.'

Louisa noticed that the ball of jade green wool lay on a small table over which was a row of switches; the lady had a telephone mouthpiece clamped to the front of her jumper, which was also jade green.

'But I came for the fire engine, I cycled, we *must* have pumps!'

'Sorry, dear, nothing I can do till one of them comes back. Even my Dad's had to go out with them tonight, that's why I'm standing by for him here. He's usually on the switchboard himself, but seeing they're all volunteers and half of them have got their own floods—'

'But it's terribly important, what shall I do?'

'Isn't there anyone else at home?'

'Yes, but only—'

'How high was it when you left?'

'Oh I don't know, inches, a foot – it was pouring in; it may be two feet by now.'

'The rain seems to have stopped,' said the wool-shop lady, peering out of the window.

'I know, but—'

'Two feet's nothing, dear. There's a house over the common said they were up to the windows; that'll take a bit of pumping out. Drat this wool, it will get round the mouthpiece.'

Louisa stood frantic while the lady untangled green wool, then dropped the ball, which rolled across the office.

'Oh, thank you, dear. Well, as I say, there's not very much we seem to be able to do, is there? Of course I'm sorry, it's a nasty mess, a flood; luckily I'm on the first floor, over the shop – haven't I seen you in the shop some time? Wasn't it you came in and asked for some tapestry patterns? I was ever so sorry we were out of them, I did order some in for Christmas, but you know what it is. . . .'

And all the time she was knitting, knitting as if the world stood still, floods and all, waiting for jade green jumpers. When Louisa came to think of it, she had never seen the lady in any other colour; presumably she just replaced them as they wore out.

'Then I'd better get back. But please, please will you send a fire engine as soon as one arrives? Here's the name and address.' And she scribbled them down on the telephone pad.

'Wait a minute, though,' said the lady, 'what's the

time? Good gracious me, after nine! And I left a joint in the oven; it'll be done to a cinder! Look here, dear, be a good girl and hold the fort for me, will you? It won't take me a minute to pop home and switch it down to Number One. Or even a Half,' she added. 'I did my last week's on Regulo a Half and it was ever so tender, Dad did enjoy it.' She poked the needles through the ball of wool and took off the mouthpiece.

'But I can't, I must go home—'

'Two ticks and I'll be back, I promise you: you know where I am; only just down the road.'

'But the water! I must go and help!' Louisa thought of Japhet and Edith Slater, of Rose and Oats and Winter and of there being only two buckets, and one of those deep under the stairs where they might not find it.

'I'll just show you the switches, not that you'll need them; I tell you I haven't had any incoming calls this last hour.' And before she could protest any more, Louisa was being instructed as to the operation of the switchboard; the mouthpiece was fastened to her wet raincoat.

'And even if they do ring, all you can say is wait, the same as I told you; just take the name and address, there's not a thing we can do until either Dad or Sam Tillett comes back. I'll leave my knitting; remind me it was a purl row next.'

Louisa was too much flabbergasted to speak as the

wool-shop lady took a coat off a hook, tied a pixie hood round her chin and hurried out, saying she'd be back in a jiff.

We ought, perhaps, in fairness to the lady, to remind you that Louisa did look more than fourteen; bus conductors often took her for sixteen at least and asked questions about the fare; and once at a party she had been offered gin with her orange, as if she were grown-up. She was certainly big for her age. All the same, it was a bit much, she thought, to be left in charge of a whole Fire Station, even a small one, on a night like this. At any other time it might have been an adventure, but now . . . She sat miserably staring at the switchboard, and even toyed with the idea of undoing all the jade green knitting by way of revenge. But no: what good would that do? She might ring up Edith Slater to explain, to ask how things were going: but no again, she couldn't get through.

Just as she was suffering an agony of frustration, annoyance and growing alarm, there was a loud buzz. Somebody was ringing! She snatched up the head-phones from the table, and with the other hand wildly pressed down switches, starting from left to right.

'Hallo, hallo, hallo,' she kept saying, 'hallo, hallo, it's no good, we can't help you; hallo, hallo, you'll have to wait—'

'Hallo!' boomed a voice in her ear. She nearly

jumped out of her wet skin. She had pressed the right switch!

'This is the Fire Station,' she said, feeling suddenly responsible.

'Hallo! Fire Station? This is Hood's Corner, Fell Common; please come immediately, as many men as you can spare, it's urgent!'

'I'm very sorry, we have no one here at all at the moment.'

'What's that? Hallo! I can't hear you. I said Hood's Corner, did you get me?'

'Yes, I got you—'

'H, double O, D—'

'Yes, I know, but you see the engines are both out. I'm terribly sorry, but if you have a flood, I'm afraid so have a lot of other people. As a matter of fact—'

'Flood!' shouted the voice. 'This is a fire! My barn's alight!'

'Did you say fire?' asked Louisa, amazed.

'Of course I said fire. What d'you think I'm ringing the Fire Station for?'

'Are you absolutely sure it's not a flood?' said Louisa, dazed but quite polite.

The voice seemed to explode. 'What? What's that? Look here, will you please put me on to somebody in charge?'

'*I* am in charge,' said Louisa. And she suddenly realized quite fully that she was; the thought made her feel strangely calm. This voice was altogether too hysterical.

'I tell you we're on fire!' it bellowed. 'Come at once!'

'We can't. And *I* tell *you*,' she added, 'that most people are flooded out, including me, only I'm not there.'

'What? I can't hear you!'

'It's been raining,' said Louisa patiently, 'and there are floods. You are quite lucky, really.' She was determined that even if the voice had lost its head, she would keep hers.

There was a crack and an exclamation in her ear, then silence. The voice had rung off. Carefully she wrote down the address; at that moment the wool-shop lady came back – so did a fire engine.

'Ah! That'll be Dad! I know the sound, that engine's the old one; we call her Grandma. Well, dear, now perhaps we'll be able to help *you* out, I always say one good turn deserves another.'

Louisa did think that fire engines were not really there to exchange good turns; but she conscientiously gave the name of Hood's Corner; she must leave it to the staff of the Fire Station to decide who had prior claim.

'Though I did come first,' she said, 'and I shouldn't think a fire would get very far in all this wet; I mean to say, going by our bonfire last Guy Fawkes. . . .'

The problem was solved by the return of Sam Tillett with the grand-daughter fire engine at that very moment. So there was a great backing and turning and hasty checking of equipment, and the two engines set out in different directions: one to a fire, the other to a flood, with Louisa sitting by Grandma's driver.

'And thank you, dear,' said the wool-shop lady, 'you were a Trojan. And it was just done to a turn, I took it out!'

'Good,' said Louisa rather grimly. Her mind was once more full of buckets and mops.

'Well, bye-bye, and good luck, oh and *which* row was it?'

'Purl!' shouted Louisa above the noise of the engine starting up.

On the drive home she reflected that village life was a strange mixture: floods and kittens and jade green jumpers; you never knew what would happen next. . . .

Meanwhile, Japhet and Edith Slater were hard at work. Edith, as soon as it really dawned on her that this was an emergency, suddenly set to and showed willing to do anything, anyhow, as fast as she could. Being Edith, this was not very fast: for instance, when she snatched an overall off a hook on the kitchen door, she stopped to do up all the buttons and to remark gently that one was missing, and that if only somebody had told her she would have sewn it on, she never minded doing her little bit to help. . . . Still, Japhet was quite surprised at her energy; she seemed to be enjoying herself nearly as much as he was.

He had fetched the large garden-broom from outside; he armed himself with this and gave Edith the smaller house one out of the kitchen cupboard. Together they swept the water frantically out of the play-room door, but as fast as they swept it came flowing in.

'I feel like the Sorcerer's Apprentice,' panted Edith with her hair net slipping off.

'Who was he?'

'Oh, don't you know the story?' – and Edith would have stood there leaning on her broom in the flood and told him, if she hadn't suddenly seen a ping-pong bat and a lot of tiddlywinks floating her way.

'Never mind about those,' said Japhet, 'we need buckets.'

He fetched one from the kitchen, also the new yellow mop his mother had bought for putting on floor polish. Edith swept away; she was long past thinking of whether she should have gone upstairs for her galoshes, or of how the doctor had told her on no account to get cold or damp this winter if she wanted to avoid that bronchitis again.

'Isn't there another bucket?' she asked. Japhet had started to bale out, tearing to and fro to empty the water outside well away from the door.

'Only the coal-scuttle.'

'Better than nothing.'

'Try the mop: dab and squeeze.'

'If it was only dabbing,' said Edith wistfully. She plunged the mop into the water and waded out with it.

'This will be so slow,' she said. 'I wish I could have a bucket.' At that moment the head of the mop came off and sank.

'Oh all right,' said Japhet, and went for the coal scuttle.

'I say!' he gasped, 'we'll have to hurry, it's all going in there now,' – pointing back to the sitting-room.

Edith snatched the coal-scuttle and began to bale like a maniac.

'We'd better rescue that best carpet,' said Japhet.

'One must do that and the other this,' – Edith was not now to be separated from her coal-scuttle.

'I'll yell if I need help,' said Japhet, and dashed away. The carpet was already sodden; he rolled it up as best he could, remembering that the wood-blocks under and around it had been repaired and waxed only that last summer. He supposed that all this water would at any rate give them a good clean; they'd probably be more golden than ever.

'Thank goodness you're back,' panted Edith, 'this is a two-man job, one to empty and one to scoop. If you stood at the door and I passed you the buckets, we could make a chain-gang.'

'Good idea.' So they organized themselves into a chain of two, which meant that Edith was deeper in water round the legs, but Japhet became wetter all over, as part of his time was spent out in the rain, emptying.

'I vote we change over,' he said some minutes later.

'Very well.'

'You know we *are* getting rid of it,' he said cheerfully as he came inside. 'It was up to that bulge on the table-leg before, now it's only just past the chipped bit.'

'And to think,' said Edith, 'that I once went in for water-divining.'

'One coming up,' Japhet called, swinging the bucket. 'Water *what*?'

'Divining. With a forked stick. It twitches.'

'Why?'

'When there's water under the ground.'

'What would it do here? Turn somersaults?' Japhet grinned and passed the coal-scuttle.

'The rain seems to be stopping,' Edith said, 'or perhaps I'm just getting used to it.'

'There's still an awful lot under the piano,' said Japhet. 'We might have to get the dust-pan.'

'Or long-handled spoons.' Japhet thought this a poor idea, but said nothing; Edith was at least entering into the spirit of the thing.

'We could try great wads of newspaper,' he said; his father did that when he de-frosted the fridge, leaving them in the bottom overnight. But that was for water dripping down; this water rose: newspapers would just be submerged.

Together they baled and mopped and swept and baled again, too busy to speak much, but both, if the truth must be told, perfectly happy. Japhet loved any active operation that was out of the ordinary; he loved thinking of new ways of doing things; secretly, and without being at all unkind, he loved disasters. So did Edith, as long as they didn't hurt animals. Besides, it wasn't her house and furniture; she was more interested than really dismayed.

So they worked away together in good accord, and as the rain eased they began to see some results; the water was inches less than it had been, and the stream that had rushed down the side of the house was reduced to a muddy trickle. Japhet had another idea: he fetched a spade and dug a channel to divert the flow so that it ran under Mrs Tucker's hedge.

Then they started with the brooms again. This worked better now, and they actually did so well as to be able to swab with torn-up pieces of old pyjama that Japhet had found under the stairs. They were doing this when his parents came home.

'What on earth? . . .' began his mother.

'Who did this?' said his father.

'Nobody, we've had a flood.'

'A real one,' Edith added, 'but Puddy's quite safe.'

They explained about the cloudburst, and how the water had flowed in; the horrified parents looked at the sitting-room, started to move furniture, asked why ever they hadn't rung up.

'You knew where we were.'

'Louisa tried, but it was out of order; she's gone for the Fire Brigade.'

'But that was a long time ago,' said Edith anxiously.

'*Gone?* In the dark? In this weather?' Their father was exceedingly startled.

'Oh, she took the bike,' said Japhet comfortably.

'But where's Rose?' their mother asked. 'In bed?'

'No, she went out to find my – oh. That was a long time ago, too.' Japhet and Edith Slater looked at each other. They had both completely forgotten about Rose!

'She went to get my boots,' said Japhet rather faintly.

'With Oats.' Edith's eyes grew round. 'Oh dear, that poor dog, I do hope—'

'You let her go out by herself?' their mother gasped.

'Only just round by the back door,' said Japhet. 'Where my boots were. I told her I didn't need them, but—'

'She's not there now,' their father said grimly.

'When was this?'

Japhet and Edith looked at each other again.

' "Underhill Trail" was still on.'

'Time does pass so,' Edith said helplessly.

'And Louisa gone too!'

'And the phone out of order.' The parents looked distraught in different ways, one nearly in tears, the other so dark with anxiety that he seemed quite angry.

'We did save the rugs,' said Japhet. 'We did our best.' He felt that after all that work he deserved a more encouraging welcome. Rose was a nuisance.

'They'll both catch their deaths of cold,' said their mother. 'Pneumonia!'

'The point is, where are they?' their father demanded.

The chain-gang of two stood silent, wet and depressed.

Then there was a knock at the back door.

Chapter Twelve

'I BROUGHT her back,' said David.

He stood blinking; a large piece of pink sticking-plaster joined his spectacles together over his nose.

Rose stood by him in blue dressing-gown, pyjamas, wellington boots and mud.

'Whatever happened?' said her mother, and pulled her in, mud and all. 'I'll make you a hot drink. You'd better have one too,' she added to David.

'What of?' asked Rose, fussy even in an emergency.

'I can't really stay,' said David, coming in. 'We're under water.'

'So are we,' said Japhet, 'or were. How much have you got?'

'We've had to move upstairs, it was up to the windows.'

'We had things floating,' said Japhet, a little taken aback.

'Drinking-chocolate or tomato soup?' said his

mother. His father went back to the play-room. Edith concentrated on Oats, and began to wipe the mud off him with newspaper out of the bottom of the airing-cupboard.

'Well, what happened?' insisted Rose's mother. 'Where have you been? We were worried stiff.'

'Were you?' said Rose, surprised.

'Of course.'

'But I haven't been long.'

'You've been hours!'

'Have I?' If Louisa had been there, she would have remarked that Rose had no sense of time at all; but of course Louisa was – well, we shall see.

'Were you more worried than if all your best china had got broken?' asked Rose.

'What an extraordinary – of *course*!'

'I'll have soup,' said Rose, pleased.

'Anyway, we haven't got any best china,' said Japhet.

This is what had happened.

Rose and Oats were searching about by the back door when Oats started to bark.

'Quiet, Oats,' said Rose, 'what is it?'

Oats told her by dashing down the drive, towards the road.

'Oats!' she yelled, 'come back!' But he didn't, so she went after him.

You may think this was a stupid thing to do, in the

pouring rain, with pyjamas on; but since they had become inseparable it seemed to Rose the most natural act in the world: Oats followed her, she followed Oats – that was all there was to it.

In the road was a wavering light; a golden light, that swung as it moved. It looked misty through the rain; Rose thought of will o' the wisps, of somebody who had said they had seen an angel – she even thought for a second of fairies. Oats simply thought that whatever it was, it shouldn't be there.

He chased it.

'Get off!' shouted a voice. 'Get out of it!'

Rose chased Oats. She saw that the lamp was swinging from a bicycle; she also saw that Oats was after the cyclist's legs. She stood at the end of the drive and shrieked: no good. Oats was barking too loudly to hear, and the man was shouting at Oats. Rose knew that if only she could get near enough, Oats would probably take notice of her; so off she went.

And what's more, off she went on going – clomping down the middle of the road, calling all the time: she had quite forgotten Japhet's boots.

The man rode on; Oats kept snapping and yapping; the man kicked out, the lamp swung perilously from side to side. Rose remembered her father saying that Oats would cause an accident on that road one of these days, and that if he did, he'd have to be put away. The very thought of such a thing made her run all the faster and call all the more shrilly; but still they went on.

What spirit of obstinacy possessed Oats that night nobody ever knew; Edith said afterwards that of course he was really asking for help; 'He knew we were in trouble,' she said, 'and he thought, "Ah, a man!"'

But whatever Oats thought took him – and Rose – skeltering down the dark road, regardless of wet, of time, of anything but following that light. Past the bus stop, round the bend, through the enormous puddles between drenched bramble bushes they went – until they came within sight of the cottage on the common. The cottage that lay low, along a track that was muddy even at the best of times. Here the man would normally have dismounted and pushed – but with Oats at his ankles he decided to try to pedal on. This was much slower work: the slush acted as a brake, and Oats panted, heaving up and down like a porpoise.

There was a sharp click, and the light wobbled violently.

'Drat you!' said the man, 'now my chain's broken!' Oats pranced about and seemed to be trying to bite the lamp; Rose saw him wagging his tail.

'He thought that at last he'd made himself clear,' said Edith afterwards.

But again, what Oats thought mattered less than what happened. The man – Mr Browne – began to push his bicycle through the thickening mud towards

123

the cottage. Oats followed; Mr Browne shouted; Oats jumped up at him, grinned and wagged his tail more. The lower the track fell, the nearer the cottage, the deeper the mud. Deeper until it was no longer mud but water. The bicycle wheels were half-submerged; Oats was swimming.

'Help!' yelled Rose. 'Help! I'm in a pond!'

The man heard her for the first time. He unhooked the Tilley lamp from the handle-bars and held it high.

'Anyone there?'

'Yes, me.'

'Who? Where?' He could see nothing but the rain blowing across the rays of the lamp.

'Me, here!' Rose panted; she had to drag her feet with all her might to prevent her wellingtons from being sucked off.

Mr Browne saw a small struggling figure appear round the nearest bush.

'This your dog?' he said.

'Yes, I tried to call him home. Oats! You're a bad boy!'

'He's a confounded pest. As if I hadn't got enough on my hands—'

'I'm sinking,' said Rose.

'You'd better go back.'

'I can't, I'm stuck.' Rose was suddenly frightened; she couldn't move either boot. 'Help!' She was nearly in tears.

'Hold on.' Mr Browne laboriously turned the bicycle round and pushed it back towards her; he couldn't let go of it, or it would have disappeared under water. Oats paddled back to her too; in the beam of the lamp his chin showed pointing anxiously upwards, with his set smile.

'What the blazes d'you think you're doing out here, a night like this?' When Mr Browne came up to her and realized her size, he was quite alarmed.

'You can't go back by yourself,' he said. 'And I can't take you, I've got a flood.'

'So have we,' said Rose, who had nearly forgotten, so intent had she been on Oats.

'Get up on the saddle,' said Mr Browne, 'you'd better come along till we can sort this out.'

'I want to hold Oats's collar, he might drown!'

'Not him,' said Mr Browne sourly; 'those sort of dogs never do.'

'He isn't a sort, he's a mongrel.'

'That's what I mean. Here, you'll have to hang on to the lamp, this is going to be stiff work.'

So Rose clutched the lamp, Mr Browne pushed and waded, Oats paddled; and after some wet, struggling minutes they came to the cottage. A light shone in an upstairs window.

'That means he's had to move out of the kitchen,' said Mr Browne. 'I thought as much. It lies too low, that's what it is; the whole place lies too low.'

Grimly he propped the bicycle against the back door and carried Rose into the dark passageway. Oats still had to swim, but the stairs were just inside, and as soon as he found a paw on the third step he scrambled up to the landing and gave himself a tremendous shake. His feet slithered outwards on the lino, his ears flapped, he spattered muddy water all over the walls and on to the two below.

'That you, Dad?' said a voice. David appeared, owl-like, from the front bedroom. 'Are they coming? It's nearly up to the top of the dresser down there.'

'You don't have to tell me. I couldn't get through. So that's fourpence gone.'

'What, not to the Fire Station?'

'Not to anyone. The box was out of order. Daft, thinking of fourpence with all this damage,' he added to himself.

'Oh, did you try the Fire Station too?' asked Rose.

'Who's she?' said David, peering down the stairs.

'That's her dratted dog; as if things weren't bad enough.'

'Oh, I know *him*,' David said. 'Are you the one who wants to be a singer?'

'I'm not really sure,' said Rose. 'I might be that first, and then a ballet dancer, if my legs get thinner. Or a ballet dancer first, I sometimes change my mind.'

'So do I,' David said interestedly, 'but it's generally teaching.' He leaned on one elbow over the banisters as if this were the most ordinary conversation to have in the middle of a flood. Rose thought so too. Mr Browne didn't.

'Well, don't just stand there,' he said. 'You'd better come down and take her back before it's any worse. We don't want her and the dog on top of everything else.'

'I was nearly not on top,' said Rose, 'I was nearly underneath.'

'If you think it's a joking matter—' began Mr Browne.

'I don't. I can only swim ten strokes, and not in a dressing-gown.'

'All my Latin books are soaked,' said David. 'I've put them out on the bed.'

'Latin!' snorted Mr Browne. 'That all you can think of?'

'No; the algebra's quite dry, it was on the draining-board—'

'For goodness' sake, at a time like this! Here, come on down, get your coat and see her home. *And* the dog.'

'Oh, Oats'll come if I do,' said Rose, 'won't you, Oats?'

He looked down from the landing, expectant.

They left Mr Browne standing gloomily in his flooded kitchen. David pushed the bicycle; Rose was now quite used to keeping her feet up and her dressing-gown tucked in; she held an electric torch – Mr Browne wouldn't be parted from the Tilley lamp.

Halfway across the common she dropped the torch, and it was lost in the mud. But David didn't seem particularly put out; he didn't go on at her as other people would.

'We could find our way by the stars,' he said, 'only there aren't any.'

'Oats knows the way.' Rose was quite confident now. 'Home, Oats,' she said. 'Why doesn't your father have a proper bicycle lamp? My sister does.'

'He's funny about some things. It's no good arguing. There are just certain things – well, he's funny, that's all. *I* don't mind,' David added, thinking perhaps he had sounded too critical. 'After all, he's my Dad. And he does want me to go to University; he's not funny about that.'

By this time they were on the proper road; it had stopped raining, the bicycle wheeled smoothly, and Oats was trotting just ahead, a light smudge in the dark. Rose and David talked about University, which Rose had heard of before, and which she now thought she might consider if her legs did not get thinner. They talked contentedly about this and that: school and food and dogs and the best position to read in bed: about pretty well everything except their floods.

Rose thought David was quite a nice boy, for a boy;

David didn't think about Rose at all; he just pushed on, hoping his Latin books would dry.

They were on their second helping of tomato soup when Louisa arrived.

'Would you believe it,' she announced in a mixture of exasperation and triumph, 'they *broke down*!'

For a fire engine to do this was Louisa's idea of the last straw. It had happened at that bridge, and for some minutes she had despaired of their ever getting out of the water at all. The wool-shop lady's Dad had sloshed about muttering that Grandma had had it; everyone had had to heave and shove; somebody said they wouldn't be surprised if the bridge collapsed.

And now that they had at last churned up her own drive – it was too late!

'I'm afraid it's hardly a job for the pumps,' said her father.

'We've done it ourselves.' Japhet looked pleased.

'With the coal-scuttle,' Edith explained proudly.

'Oh well,' the firemen said, 'in that case . . .'

'I expect you'd like a cup of something?' Louisa's mother asked, looking at the four men resignedly. They were very large men, and Japhet had drunk all but the last pint of milk.

But the wool-shop lady's Dad said thank you all the same, they'd better get back as they might be wanted elsewhere.

'May I *see* your flood?' David asked politely.

'Certainly,' said Rose, and made for the play-room, trailing blankets.

'Come back,' said her mother, 'your hair's not dry, you'll get pneumonia.' She had been trying to manipulate the hair dryer with one hand and stir soup with the other; the flex was not long enough and Rose still had half a wet fringe.

Louisa went with them to inspect the damage.

'It's not half as bad as ours,' said David. 'Not a tenth as bad. We're up to the windows.'

'No one's to use the sitting-room,' said their father, 'until it's dried out.'

'What about telly?' Japhet was dismayed.

'Are you really up to the windows?' Louisa asked, looking at David with much concern.

'Yes, and Dad couldn't even get through to a fire engine.'

'Have ours!' Louisa suggested benevolently. Even as she said it, she thought it sounded rather odd to be offering somebody a fire engine; but after all, wasn't it the obvious thing to do?

'We don't need it now and you do,' she said, 'so why not tell them, quickly?'

'Dad would be glad,' said David, suddenly conscience-stricken at the thought of his father alone in all that water, and himself here surrounded by people and full of soup.

So they rushed out and stopped Grandma's driver just as he was backing into the road; and at last, thought Louisa, they were able to do the mushroom man some sort of a good turn.

In fact, it was a very good turn indeed; that low-lying cottage might have been uninhabitable to this day if it had not been for the pumps. David's algebra was saved just in time; his Latin dried out; Mr Browne thanked his lucky stars that the kitchen had a brick floor and that he had left his best boots on the dresser. The lilac and the last year's Christmas cards didn't matter: on second thoughts, he realized with something of a surprise, nothing mattered but that the child and her dog had been there that night and had led to his unexpected rescue. In less than half an hour the water was reduced from thigh-level to a mere sludge underfoot; Mr Browne looked round and was grateful. So grateful, indeed, that he – but no; it's too soon to say what he did.

The chief thing to mention now is that it was not Rose who got pneumonia; it was Edith Slater. And in a few days she was so bad that the doctor ordered her to be moved to the local hospital, where she would not be tempted to struggle out of bed every time Oats scratched at her door.

You may not think that there could be much connection between Edith Slater's pneumonia and Japhet's tea-pot; but you need not be Louisa to know that connections can be very peculiar.

Even romantic.

Even dramatic.

Anyway, as peculiar as people themselves.

Chapter Thirteen

IT was three weeks since the night the rain came in, and they were all to visit Edith Slater at the cottage hospital. Or rather, their mother was to visit as usual, possibly with Louisa; Rose and Japhet would have to wait outside.

'I don't think it's fair,' complained Rose, 'not allowing children.'

'I'm going to take her some flowers out of my garden,' said Japhet. He was really sorry for Edith, and after that night when they had baled together he felt a special bond with her. He put on his boots and tramped out into the November afternoon.

'I don't believe he's got any flowers in his garden,' said Louisa. 'I haven't, and I look after mine much more than he does.'

But Japhet came back with a bunch of scraggy chrysanthemums, and a kilner jar that he had found in the chicken-house.

'This wants washing,' he said, and started to make a terrible mess in the sink.

Their mother told them all to hurry up. Louisa, in honour of the occasion, put on her best grey Sunday coat; Rose was made to wear an extra cardigan underneath and her father's huge black and red scarf on top. Louisa told her she looked like a refugee; their mother said better that than to be frozen. She went about muttering in a harassed way that it was a pity it happened to be a Saturday afternoon when their father was out; it would have been so much easier to have left them all at home; as it was, there was the boiler to do, and that kitten to be shut in the play-room, where it slept in an old bicycle basket, and the house to be locked up. . . .

'Do come on,' she said to Japhet.

'Where's Oats?' asked Louisa, looking ready and very respectable.

'I don't know, and we can't bother with him now.'

'We *must* find him,' protested Rose, 'we can't leave him just loose.'

Their mother pointed out that that was what he generally was, and that it was entirely his own fault.

At last they started; the two girls in the back of the car, Japhet in the front because it was his turn.

The afternoon was nasty, cold and damp. 'It's going to be foggy tonight,' said their mother, concentrating on the road. 'I'm glad Edith's safe and warm.'

'How long d'you think they'll keep her in there?' Louisa was asking when suddenly Rose shrieked, 'There's Oats!'

'Right in my ear,' said their mother, wincing.

'Stop, stop!' Japhet bounced in the front seat and let down the window. He and Rose yelled at Oats, who saw them and came streaking across the sodden common. Japhet burst out laughing; Oats looked such a frantic and delighted dog.

'Oh let him in, let him in!' they begged. 'Poor old dog, he wants to come.'

Oats ran so near the car that their mother had to stop anyway, and abruptly.

Japhet opened the door; in flew a scuffle of wagging and mud.

'All over my best coat!' wailed Louisa. 'Look what he's done! Why can't you *hold* him?' She was red in the face with indignation at Japhet, who sat rocking with laughter as Oats's wild tail tickled his ear.

'Here, my feet are all wet,' said their mother. 'What's this pool?'

'Dash, they must have tipped over when you stopped,' Japhet said. The kilner jar was lying on its side on the floor by the driver's seat; the two rubber foot-mats were under water.

'Never mind,' said Japhet.

'I do mind. It's all in my shoes.'

'Fancy bringing them in a jar of water,' said Louisa.

'Really, some people! You're as bad as June Barrow and the jelly.'

'Well, I wanted them to keep fresh, didn't I?' It was Japhet who was indignant now.

'What jelly?' asked Rose.

'Oh, we had to take food to school for a party, and she brought a jelly on a plate, *turned out*. It was wobbling all over the place in the wind.'

'You take flowers to people in paper, not water,' said Rose.

'You aren't even taking any at all,' Japhet retorted, and their mother had to start the car up before there was any more argument.

They parked against the wall of the hospital, which was a low red-gabled building with a short asphalt drive and some flower-beds chained off between white posts. Edith was on the ground floor, but the window was so high that only Louisa and her mother could see over the edge without jumping. Edith was there in a blue bed-jacket, gazing into space. In the bed next to her a very old lady was playing draughts with a man in a raincoat.

'Now you wait here,' said their mother to Japhet and Rose. 'And if you get cold, sit in the car.'

Oats desperately wanted to go into the hospital too; Louisa told Japhet for goodness' sake to hold his collar; they hadn't brought the lead.

'I want to look through the window,' said Rose when

Louisa and her mother were inside. 'Will you lift me up?'

'I'll have to tie him somewhere,' Japhet said, dragging Oats to the boot of the car.

'Put him in.'

'No, he hates that, and he'll scrabble all over the seats,' said Japhet with unusual forethought. It was more fun to find an old rope from under the back seat and rig up a tether from Oats to the chain rail. Having done this, Japhet obligingly hoisted Rose up to a tiny foothold on the wall, where she could cling to the window ledge and see in. She grinned and waved to Edith Slater, who eventually smiled wanly and waved back. The old lady in the other bed waved too.

'My turn,' said Japhet, and let Rose go so that she scraped her knees and the toes of her shoes on the bricks. She complained bitterly, but her voice was unheard above the agitated yapping of Oats, who was going nearly mad with anxiety to join in.

The old lady saw Japhet's pink face at the window and said something to the man in the raincoat. He leaned forward to the cupboard by her bed and then came to the window with a round tin.

'Mrs Birch says to have one.' He opened the window just enough to put the tin through the crack; Japhet took a fruit-drop.

'And one for the little girl.' Japhet took another.

'Thank you,' he said. The old lady was watching;

she seemed to be saying something as the man shut the window. He opened it again.

'She says to take a handful. Only I can't hold it long on account of the draught.'

Japhet beamed at Mrs Birch; then he told Rose to give Oats a fruit-drop to keep him quiet. But Oats swallowed it at a gulp, and went on yapping more than ever. Rose demanded her turn again at the window.

'And this time don't let me go so suddenly.'

She clung to the ledge with her finger-nails; Mrs Birch saw her anxious face bob up, with shoulders hunched, as Japhet heaved from behind. Suddenly Oats choked. Japhet rushed off to pat. him; Rose yelled, 'Ow!'; Mrs Birch, hearing nothing, just saw the fringe disappear as suddenly as it had arisen.

'That your brother and sister?' she said to Louisa, who had for the moment run out of invalid conversation.

'Yes; they're not allowed in.'

'Tell 'em there's a little ladder in the lobby there, just by the entrance. Go on! Nobody'll mind.'

'Are you sure?'

'Course. Prop it up at the winder, they'll be all right. It's only a little one. You tell 'em.'

Louisa looked at her mother, who only shrugged. There was another twenty minutes visiting time to go, and glad as she was to see Edith, she was still more glad of any small mercy, even a ladder, which would check the goings-on of Japhet and Rose and Oats outside.

Louisa found the lobby, which contained a wheel-chair, a glass-fronted bookcase with musty-looking volumes called things like *Up the Amazon*, *Famous Tales of Horror* and *Lelia – a Romance* – and, in a corner, the small step-ladder.

Doubtfully she carried it out and was greeted by renewed yelpings from Oats, exclamations of delight from Japhet, and cries of, 'He just doesn't care!' from Rose, who was dabbing tears and a bloody knee alternately with the old wash-leather from the car.

Louisa tried to pacify them all by setting up the ladder under the window. She was just making sure it was firm when a loud sharp voice said:

'What's going on out here?'

They all turned round guiltily; all except Oats, who went on barking heedlessly. Hospital Sisters meant nothing to him.

'And what do you imagine you're doing?' Louisa knew at once that this must be Sister Andrews; Edith had been telling them how she was the terror of the hospital.

'We were just – I mean, they wanted to see in. Well, we were told we could.'

'Who told you?' snapped Sister Andrews. She snatched the step-ladder and folded it up.

'Oh, somebody,' mumbled Louisa. She wasn't going to give away old Mrs Birch.

'Well, you've no business. This is hospital property.'

'I'm sorry,' said Louisa; then, recovering her calm and feeling rather cross: 'But the window's too high. It wouldn't have been necessary otherwise. After all, a ground floor should *be* a ground floor.'

Sister Andrews glared at her for a moment, wondering if she had heard aright. No one had ever dared to argue with her before. She opened her mouth to speak, but Oats set up such an ear-splitting racket that she thought better of it, and simply marched off with the step-ladder.

'Old beast,' said Japhet.

'Poor Edith, being nursed by *her*,' said Rose.

'I dare say her bark's worse than her bite.' Louisa tried to be fair. Then she went in to say good-bye to Edith; it was nearly time to go.

Japhet's chrysanthemums were still lying on the bed; on top of Edith's locker was a tiny bunch of violets in a fish paste pot. Edith did not mention these, but said, 'Tell Japhet they'll put his in water when you've gone. And thank you very much for coming to see me.'

'Not at all,' said Louisa cheerfully, 'I did it for sheer pleasure.'

Edith smiled with the held-back, very bright-eyed smile that Louisa never quite understood; she had seen it on grown-ups' faces before. But it didn't matter; she *was* pleased that she had come, and had determined that even after Edith Slater left the hospital it might be a good idea sometimes to visit old Mrs Birch, who apparently would be there for life. Louisa thought this very sad, almost unimaginable; besides, she had watched the game of draughts out of the corner of her eye, and decided that the old lady ought to be allowed sometimes to win.

They arrived home through gathering fog to a cold house, a remotely miaouwing kitten, dusk and the boiler low and no sitting-room where a fire could be lit. It had been severely shut up since the night of the rain, awaiting redecoration. Their father had kept an electric fire on in there for hours at a time, but the drying-out seemed so slow that he said he couldn't afford all this current and things had better be left to nature.

Which is how Japhet found them.

Of course he shouldn't have gone in there at all really; they had all been told to keep out in case they knocked down any lumps of damp plaster or generally made things worse.

But Japhet was terribly fed up with the arrangement for watching TV in the so-called dining-room. This was really little more than a wide brick passage, and they all had to sit huddled on cushions on the floor, with Rose and Oats continually stepping over everybody because they wanted to go and do something else; Japhet couldn't even put a bottle of milk down safely. And Louisa took up too much room anyway, apart from always trying to knit or write or do huge drawings as well as look; so she grumbled with extra sourness about spilt milk. In fact they had had a very uncomfortable three weeks' watching.

Accordingly, and as he thought in particular how nice it would be to see 'Scarface' again in comfort, Japhet went to investigate the prospects of getting the TV moved back to its old place in the sitting-room.

'Hi!' he shouted. 'Hey! Come here! Look what's happened!'

'It's all loose,' said Rose slowly, gazing at the floor. 'It's all come to pieces.'

'It's shrunk,' said Louisa with a more scientific approach. 'The wood blocks must have swelled with the wet, then shrunk back again.'

'They shrunk too much,' said Rose. She looked at them reproachfully.

'Look, they come up.' Japhet lifted a block out of its place.

'Put that back,' said Louisa, 'or it might never fit again.'

'I don't see how they'll *ever* get them back,' Japhet said, not at all worried. 'We'd better have concrete.'

'In the sitting-room? By the way, I wonder how that

poor mushroom man – I mean Mr Browne – got on. His place sounded much worse than ours.'

'Oh, they're all right,' said Japhet. 'I asked David at the bus stop. He says it's dried up a bit and everything was saved. His father's asked for another cottage, though. I told him about Edith too,' he added, 'he seemed sorry.'

'What d'you mean, asked for another cottage?'

'Oh I don't know, something to do with the farm—'

'Look!' Rose interrupted them with a great squeak. She was on her knees on the broken floor. Between a finger and thumb she held up something pinkish and whitish and roundish, on a short stalk.

'Mushrooms!' Louisa gaped.

'My tea-pot!' shouted Japhet, and dived for the hearth. The tea-pot lay on its side, lid off, some way away from the place where he had left it.

'It must have floated,' he said, 'and got washed up here with the flood.'

He looked inside; the pot was empty except for a grimy sediment mixed with bits of fluff off the carpet.

'. . . I've made toasted cheese if you want it,' came a resigned voice from the kitchen. 'And have you hung your coats up, or—'

They rushed to tell their mother the good news, Japhet first because, after all, it was his tea-pot.

Chapter Fourteen

'I STILL SAY we don't know whether they *are* mush-rooms,' said their mother for the twentieth time. 'And even if they are, what about the sitting-room?'

'We could have the telly in my bedroom,' said Japhet brightly.

'I will not have a mushroom farm in the sitting-room,' their mother went on, 'it's the one room in the house . . .'

Their father calmed her down.

'Anyway, I shall take one to show Edith,' she said; 'she was always good at botany at school. She'll know.'

'What about the mushroom man?' Louisa asked. 'He ought to know, if anyone does.'

'I'll give one to David at the bus stop,' Japhet said. 'Then he can ask his Dad.'

'He might forget, he's always thinking about Latin.'

'Or that Podge might get it first and eat it,' said Rose.

'*I'll* take Mr Browne a sample,' said Louisa firmly.

'Well, no one here's going to eat them until we know,' their mother said. 'They might be toadstools.'

'Oh yes, all those coffins,' said Rose in her don't-tell-me-again voice. A cryptic remark to anyone outside this family; but they had listened many times with round eyes or grins, or both, to the story of a French film their mother had once seen, which started with a row of little coffins and only one small boy alive. 'And he was the only one who hadn't eaten the toadstools!' she would finish in grim triumph.

'A mushroom. Definitely a mushroom,' said Edith Slater, breaking it gently over the hospital sheet. 'And all out of Japhet's tea-pot – fancy that!'

'Don't you believe it,' said Mr Browne to Louisa, who sat with a paper bag at his kitchen table. 'Those are never mushrooms. Couldn't be. They wouldn't have had the time.'

'Why not?'

'Well, you say he left this tea-pot there the night the rain came in. Which is four weeks Saturday. A mushroom takes six to eight.'

'Oh yes,' Louisa remembered the leaflet, 'but people do go on as if they grew overnight.'

'People who haven't tried it. Of course once they start, it's quick: but they won't start till getting on for two months after spawning. Which means either these did *not* come out of the tea-pot, or they are *not* mushrooms, or both.'

'How d'you mean, both?'

'If you ask me, they're toadstools and they've been there all the time.'

'What, growing under our floor?'

'No knowing what you'll find in these damp places,' said Mr Browne darkly. 'I've known a puff-ball as big as my head, right under that dresser.'

'Oh dear,' sighed Louisa, picking up the paper bag, 'and Edith was so sure.'

'Tell her from me,' said Mr Browne, 'those are never mushrooms. Never. And my regards.'

'Tell *him* from *me*,' retorted Edith, who was much better, 'that there are over ninety different kinds of edible fungi and this is one of them. He can call it what he likes.' She was quite heated at such a challenge to her botany. 'Now mind you tell him,' she insisted. 'Don't forget. I shall ask you if you have.'

Louisa backed out of the ward thinking what strange things Edith grew excited about; rather like a child. She even looked somewhat childish, sitting up there in bed with her hair done in two pigtails. Having pneumonia seemed to have suited her; now that she was recovering, she was quite skittish, brighter-eyed and surely a little plumper. She said the rest had done her good; but she was looking forward to going back to her little room in London, and to her work for the R.S.P.C.A.

'My poor sparrows there,' she said. 'I'm sure they must all be wondering what on earth's happened.'

Louisa grinned at the thought of a sparrow wondering this. Mrs Birch caught the grin and offered fruit-drops as usual; the round tin seemed to be inexhaustible.

'I gets 'im to fill up for me, Saturdays,' she explained. ' 'E's very good.' Louisa supposed she meant the man in the raincoat, and was saddened again to think of the poor old lady stuck there with nothing to look forward to but a weekly visit, and to be beaten at draughts.

'But it's all very well,' she said to her mother, 'we can't keep *on* carrying messages to and fro about these mushrooms.'

'Toadstools.'

'Well, whatever they are. I shall tell Mr Browne that if he wants to go into it any further he'll have to write.'

'He won't like that,' said Rose ominously. She was at the kitchen table ruling a margin along a knitting-needle. She had suddenly started to have arithmetic homework; another complication in everyone's life, as it meant clearing an extra space after tea and turning out the vase for a rubber and trying to make Rose see that six sevens were more urgent than patting Oats or drawing little men round the side of the book.

'I hate writing letters,' she said. 'And anyway, some

might be mushrooms and some toadstools; they ought to try them one by one. Besides,' she added, 'it costs stamps. I thought you said he was poor.'

'Writing letters depends on how interested people are,' said Louisa judicially.

'And if they have the time,' her mother said.

It so happened that Edith, still sitting in bed, did have the time – nor was she all that poor; their mother had often said she had never known anyone with such a supply of rich old aunts. From time to time one of them died, which was just as well for Edith, though she had no idea of money and spent hardly anything on herself. But she would never have to think where the next stamp was coming from.

As for Mr Browne, he may have been short of stamps but not of interest. The interest of a professional who was suddenly being put on the spot. In fact, he was considerably annoyed that anyone should defy his authority about mushrooms. Latin, maths, French – he knew nothing about these at all, and felt secretly ashamed of his ignorance in front of David. All the more reason to dig in his heels about mushrooms.

A curious correspondence started. We won't bother you with the letters themselves; only to say that Mr Browne wrote to Edith on pieces of paper torn out of David's old exercise books, and that at first he was quite polite. He simply said would she excuse him but he had had years with mushrooms and did know what he was talking about. Edith promptly wrote back to say so did she; she even had a book at home on *The Fungi of Great Britain*.

Mr Browne wrote again to say that books were not always right. Edith replied that hers was. Mr Browne became shorter and sharper and more economical: he sent a postcard saying simply, 'Sorry have looked again they are toadstools.' This card nearly sent up Edith's temperature; she snatched a sheet of paper and scribbled in the middle of it one word: 'Mushrooms!' – then added two more exclamation marks and asked Sister Andrews please to post it at once.

The only hint Louisa had that this was going on was that Mr Browne did appear with his lamp one evening and asked to be allowed to see the sitting-room. With great surprise they unbolted it and let him in; the wood blocks were still loose, the things – whatever they were – still sprouting underneath.

'It's the second crop,' said Louisa. 'But they're supposed to be coming to do the floor soon.'

Mr Browne took one look, said nothing, and started to march out.

'I hear you may be moving,' said Louisa.

'Maybe. That place of mine should be condemned.'

'Have you found anywhere else?'

'They've got another tied cottage, over near the farm. Be empty by Christmas. Bigger, though; don't know if I could run it. Can't expect the boy to go on doing housework, now he's getting on. He needs the time for his studies. Will do, more and more.'

Mr Browne picked up the Tilley lamp and went away, unsmiling as usual.

'Poor man,' sighed Louisa, and got out her list. Or rather, the intended list: actually it was merely a paper neatly headed 'W. for M.M. – Possibilities'. Looking at it despondently, she realized that she had gone no-where, nowhere at all, towards finding Mr Browne a wife.

'What about that cake-shop lady?' suggested Rose. 'She makes lovely things.'

'Oh yes,' Japhet joined in, 'remember that enormous great Christmas cake she made last year, all covered with polar bears and little ships stuck in the snow?'

'Ice,' said Louisa. 'It was the North Pole, I asked her. She did it because she once had an uncle who went there. She would have liked to, but she had to make cakes instead, so she made that one.' Louisa had dis-covered all this for the price of six plain scones; she always liked to find out about people.

'Well, what about her? She's not married, is she?' Rose seemed to think that this and cooking were the only requirements.

'In the first place,' said Louisa with forced patience, 'she weighs about twenty-four stone; I doubt if she'd even be able to get *in* to a tied cottage.'

'I know!' Japhet lit up with inspiration. 'Miss Mc-Cormick!' If ever there were a case of killing two birds with one stone, this was surely it. Japhet wasn't all that much interested in wives for the mushroom man, but the idea of getting rid of Miss McCormick was irresistible.

'Podge'd be so happy,' he beamed.

'We're not concerned with making Podge happy,' Louisa said severely. 'What about poor David? From all we've heard, *he* wouldn't be very happy. Besides which, is she decent to look at?'

'No,' said Japhet. 'Why?'

'Well, he's not likely to want to marry anybody who doesn't look *fairly* all right. We don't want to put him off from the start.'

'Mrs Tucker—' began Rose doubtfully.

'Don't be silly,' said Louisa, 'she's about eighty and a widow and deaf; and she'd never want to leave her raspberries. They win prizes.'

'She could take them with her,' suggested Japhet. 'I wouldn't mind digging them up. I might find something buried.'

Louisa gave him one of her looks; this was just another example of Japhet's wanting to do things for his own fun and not for the real reason at all.

'There is, of course, that wool-shop lady. . . .' she murmured. 'Only she'd have to stop looking after her Dad.' But the wool-shop lady wasn't too bad an idea; she was comfortable-looking, and good-tempered, and not too old, and she'd be able to knit things. Louisa saw Mr Browne and David permanently fitted out with jade-green jumpers; she smiled faintly and put the wool-shop lady down on the list. In fact, the wool-shop lady *was* the list. Louisa sighed and felt useless; a feeling which didn't suit her at all.

At that moment – it was Sunday evening, and as dark and dank as evenings can be towards the end of November – there was a familiar scratching at the back door.

'Oats!'

They let him in; he shook himself, ears a-flap, fur wet from the fog. He had been out since before tea.

'He's got something in his mouth!'

'What is it? Drop it, boy!'

Rose was now the only one for whom Oats would drop anything. She took a sodden object out of his mouth.

'It's a cap!'

'David's cap! It is, it must be, it's a Grammar School one. He must have been all the way to that bush and found it. Good old dog, good old Oats, then!' Japhet hugged Oats and laughed.

It was Louisa, of course, who took back the cap. And

she insisted on doing it that very night, because David would want it in the morning. Her mother dithered a bit and said she didn't like her going out alone in the dark, but eventually allowed that if she went on the bike and came straight back, well, all right.

'Dad's not in,' said David, 'but I'll put it in the oven and it may dry off. Thanks. I was to have got another one, but I spent the money on – well, on something else.'

Louisa thought it rather strange that Mr Browne should be out on a Sunday evening; but when she asked if he was working, the answer was simply, 'No; he's out visiting.' So she said no more, except, 'For goodness' sake turn the oven down low; you don't want a baked peak and button and wet inside.'

David smiled like a slightly surprised owl; they said good-night as Louisa tripped over the pink shell on the doorstep.

'Well,' said their mother, 'Edith is to go home to-morrow. I do hope she'll take care of herself, but I doubt it. All I can do is take her to the station.'

'They wouldn't let her out,' said Louisa, 'unless she were really better.'

'I asked her to come back here to convalesce; but she's so wrapped up in those birds.'

'What about *our* birds?' complained Rose.

'She just says give them cheese. Anyway, the men are coming tomorrow to do that floor.'

'What's that got to do with birds?' Louisa asked.

'Oh, I don't know,' her mother sighed. She was always being trapped by Louisa's logic just when the scrambled egg was doing too hard. 'Well,' she pulled herself together defiantly, 'everything has to do with everything, if you come to think of it.'

Japhet and Rose didn't see this at all; they started mentioning things like Brussels sprouts and helicopters, which couldn't possibly be to do with each other. Their mother desperately reminded them that a farmer up the road did spray his fields by helicopter. Louisa said sharply, 'Does he grow sprouts?' But she knew that this really wasn't the point; she alone felt that her mother might be right. Things and events and people *were* connected, when you came to think of it. . . . She went to bed that night reflecting upon pictures of mushrooms and tea-pots and floods and fire engines and David's cap and Edith's birds. . . . All connected, yes: but what use was that if nothing happened? Her mushroom venture, for instance: what had that led to but a chapter of accidents and an argument? In a book, perhaps, it would have made a fortune. And tomorrow the floor would be put back just as before, and there would be only a few last damp patches to remind them of the night the rain came in; and even those would probably have gone away by next summer. She sighed, turned over and went to sleep.

Now prepare for a shock. At least you can be warned to prepare for it: Louisa's family couldn't. It came to them like a bolt from the blue.

Edith had duly departed; the floor had been put back; the first week of December had started with steady drizzle; their father had blocked the bottom of that play-room door with a huge piece of wood so that no more water could ever come in. Nothing unusual had happened, except that Miss McCormick was now sending Japhet home with intelligence tests to do, in a last wild hope of his passing the Eleven Plus in January. So their mother had three lots of homework going at the same time, and burned the ironing-board cloth to a brown tatter trying to keep pace with it all. Japhet would start off quite well, but the *amount* of questions drove him to weary recklessness, so that his eyes got smaller and smaller and his writing larger and larger; and when they asked (number forty), 'Which is farther from the earth, the moon or Mars?' He just put 'No'.

It was during such an evening, in the middle of Rose's long division, that the telegram arrived.

Perhaps it won't be a shock to you at all. Perhaps you'll think it's quite dull. Or perhaps you saw it coming all the time.

On the other hand, you may think, like Louisa, that things are connected more than we can possibly foresee – even the doings of children and of seemingly unchangeable grown-ups.

The telegram simply said that Edith Slater was engaged to the mushroom man.

Chapter Fifteen

'I HATE TO think what all these trunk calls are going to cost,' said their father as he put down the phone. 'To say nothing of the telegrams.'

'I can't help it, I feel so responsible,' their mother protested. 'Edith never did have any sense, and now . . . !'

Louisa felt responsible, too; after all, it was originally she and her mushrooms who had brought them together. And Rose, of course, going round there that night; and the flood; and the tea-pot. . . .

But as to sense, she was beginning to wonder. Edith's answers to their frantic inquiries seemed very positive. On Monday night their mother, unable to get her on the phone, had wired, 'All surprised what about the boy?' Edith's telegram came on Tuesday morning: 'Thought you would be. Nice boy. Violets.' Louisa was the one who worked out what this meant.

'He must have been to the hospital,' she said; '– yes, and *that* was what he spent his cap money on!'

157

'She's mad,' said their mother, meaning Edith.

'– And I bet that was where Mr Browne was visiting, that Sunday night! Of all the dark horses!'

'It's not even as if she can cook,' their mother went on, almost wringing her hands. 'Or anything. She's never done any proper housework in her life.'

Edith, on the telephone on Wednesday, said that she was perfectly capable of starting now, and reminded them that, after all, she had swept out a flood.

'It's not the same,' said their mother. 'And he may not like nut rissoles at all. Besides, what about all that damp? You'll never be able to live there; you'll get pneumonia all the time.'

'Tell her she might die,' said Rose.

'Rose says you might die!' their mother shouted down the line.

'He's moving out,' Edith replied calmly. 'To a nice dry place on the hill. He's told me all about it.'

'It'll be too windy,' said their mother. 'You'll get lumbago.'

'I shall wear three skirts,' said Edith, and rang off.

'She seems very determined,' their mother sighed. 'I don't know, I'm sure. It's all so quick: I can't understand how it happened.'

They never did understand. Both Edith and Mr Browne were very reserved on the subject; all *she* would say was, 'Well, those mushrooms . . .' and all *he* would say was that he had been sorry to hear about her being ill, after that flood, and he felt grateful to have come out of it so well himself, so he went along to see her one night, and that was that.

And indeed, by the end of a week of wires and phone calls, they all had to admit that it *was* that.

'And she actually wants a Christmas wedding,' said their mother, 'and Rose to be the bridesmaid.'

'Only one bridesmaid?' Louisa was a little disappointed.

'They don't want to spend too much on the dresses.'

'Let Oats be a brides-dog,' suggested Japhet, 'he wouldn't need a dress.'

'That's not funny,' said Louisa, turning away so as not to laugh. 'Weddings are serious things, dogs are not allowed.'

'Nobody would think Oats was a serious dog,' said Rose, 'even if he was.'

After that, everything happened with a rush.

'Edith is to be married from here!' their mother announced.

'What, with a real clergyman?' Japhet was impressed.

'Don't be silly, I mean she'll have the reception here. I said I'd arrange it.'

'What's a reception?' Rose asked.

'A sort of party,' Louisa told her, 'that they have afterwards, with a cake.'

'And champagne,' their father added. 'I always think it's overrated, champagne.'

'We're going to do it properly.' Their mother was firm. 'I've known Edith since we were six, at dancing class, and what's the use of that if I can't see her decently married? No one else will.'

'Hasn't she any relations at all?' Louisa asked.

'Only those old aunts; I think there are about two left, goodness knows where.'

'It won't be much of a party,' Rose said, 'with just us.'

'Couldn't I ask Georgia?' Louisa brightened. 'Her mother never takes her to weddings. They went to a terribly smart one the other day, and she was just left at home with that cook.'

'This won't be a terribly smart one,' said their mother.

'No, but couldn't I? After all, if I'm not to be a bridesmaid—'

'You'll have to help with the food,' her mother reminded her.

'Food? Can Podge come?' Japhet asked.

'Oh, not Podge!' Rose pronounced the name as if it were an outrage.

'Why not?'

'Well, there'll be David, and you, and surely that's

enough boys. We don't want the whole house bulging.'

'It wouldn't. Anyway, it's a party. And anyway, it's different for David, he's absolutely got to be there, so he doesn't count.'

'It'll be funny for him,' Louisa reflected, 'seeing his father married.'

'Oh, he doesn't mind,' Japhet said casually, 'I spoke to him at the bus stop. He's quite glad.'

'Anyway, it'll be funny for everybody,' their mother said, 'if we don't get on and do something about the arrangements. What with Christmas as well. . . .'

The next two weeks were hectic. Their mother kept tearing about in the car to and from shops; everyone had to eat standing up or sitting on the floor because the kitchen table was always covered with pastry; there was nowhere to put anything down, and the vase on the mantelpiece overflowed; Rose's arithmetic corrections had to have mincemeat wiped off; Japhet got silver paint all over the play-room floor, trying to make a fretwork horseshoe.

Only Oats and that kitten kept fairly calm; and only Louisa remembered regularly to feed them.

Their mother decided that she hadn't time to make Rose's dress as well as everything else, and there were frantic inquiries as to a quick dressmaker.

Louisa suggested the wool-shop lady.

'I don't want a *knitted* bridesmaid's dress,' said Rose

in alarm.

'She might be able to sew as well. She sells sewing things.'

Louisa was right; the wool-shop lady did sew, and was quite placid about the whole thing. Yes, she could run up a simple white costume, as she called it, in a couple of days. As long as they didn't want embroidery. Of course, she added rather wistfully, embroidery would have been nice, just a touch of colour. Little green leaves, for instance, she could do quite quickly in lazy-daisy stitch all round the neck and sleeves, it would be something unusual. . . . Their mother said firmly no embroidery, and all white, please.

'If it's to be a white wedding,' said Louisa, 'wouldn't it be nice if we had a white Christmas too? We haven't had any proper snow ever since we've lived here.'

'We could go to church by sledge!' Japhet said.

'Not in a wedding-dress.'

'Podge and I won't be wearing wedding-dresses.'

'We haven't got a sledge,' Louisa said flatly.

Their mother reminded their father to have the car serviced and filled up with petrol in good time. Edith didn't want hired cars, she said they would make her feel nervous.

Mr Browne, meanwhile, was getting on with things in his own quiet way. The wedding was arranged for

Christmas Eve: just in time to have the banns read and to move into the other cottage. The move was all done one cold dry Saturday, with the least possible fuss; Mr Browne was a determined and methodical man, even if some of his methods (such as washing-up) were peculiar.

Louisa's mother sent her round that afternoon to see if she could help; she found David and his father sitting in the new kitchen drinking tea. And by comparison with the other, it really was new – this cottage being in fact a pink brick bungalow which had only been put up a few years ago.

Louisa thought it, in a way, less appealing than the old damp place by the railway bank; but she didn't say so. Mr Browne and David seemed solemnly happy, and of course the bungalow would be much better for Edith. Dry, and not draughty, and with a nice white sink. Louisa congratulated them on moving so quickly and neatly: even the pink shell was in its new place on the cement doorstep.

On Christmas Eve it did not snow: but a thick frost singled out every leaf and grass-blade and twig and tile and gable, so that cottages and common were all one silver-white.

At half-past eight Edith was given grated apple in the little spare-room: she said it was all the breakfast she could manage, except for the cup of tea placed in the rosebud bowl. Rose and the rest of the family had been told to stay in their dressing-gowns until the last minute, in case anybody spilt anything.

Their mother had been up since six, arranging a tremendous spread of sausage-rolls and mince-pies and strange-looking cold things in bowls, to be served with wooden spoons.

There were six long French loaves to be cut up and buttered. There was a crate of champagne and Coca-Cola to be put out in the frost to keep chilled. Japhet did this. There was Rose's wreath to be fastened to two hair-slides (from the vase), otherwise it might fall off. There were the Christmas tree lights to be seen to – their father's job – because one of them always fused at the last minute.

'It's funny,' said Rose, 'to have a Christmas tree *and* a wedding-cake. I don't know which to look at most.'

Indeed, in all its three or four hundred years, that little brick-floored dining-room had probably never been so crammed with festivity. In one corner stood the tree, hung with silver balls and strings of gold beads – Louisa had found these beads at the local stationer's in all colours; she had been tempted to have red and green and blue as well, but was now glad that she had kept to silver and gold. There was the green of the tree, and the red of the candles on the window-sill, in white china candlesticks wound round with tinsel. On the sideboard were glasses, food, and the best of the Christmas cards. On the table, more food; and in the centre, so high that it seemed almost to touch the rough daubed plaster ceiling – the cake. Three tiers, as white as the frost outside, with a silver board underneath and silver bells on top. The cake-shop lady had made it as a special favour; she was so booked up with Christmas things that at first she had refused, shaking all her double chins in hopelessness. But Louisa had pleaded, their mother had looked woe-begone, Rose had stared across the counter in silent gloom, and Japhet had said, 'I suppose we'll have to do without a cake, then. I thought it might be the *South* Pole this time; it *is* it's turn.'

In the end, the cake-shop lady had sighed, fingered her amber beads and lumbered off in her huge white overall 'To See'.

From the dim and spicy back regions of her shop she had reappeared with what she called her Special Book. Crumbs fell out of it; she breathed heavily, poring over its entries, which were here and there made illegible by lard or pink icing-sugar.

'Would you want decorations?' she asked. 'Polar bears? Eskimos?'

Their mother said no bears, this was a wedding-cake.

'Icicles?' the cake-shop lady asked hopefully, still breathing into the Book.

'Well, just as you think,' said their mother, half-meek and half-triumphant. She knew she had won the day, and she wouldn't like to deprive anyone of icicles.

'Would you be able to eat them?' asked Rose, and the cake-shop lady gave her a look as much as to say, 'Do you imagine I would ever make an uneatable icicle?'

So there was the cake. Not, as it turned out, with icicles, but with circles of little white pillars, each supported – to the family's delight – by a tiny sugar seal; its flippers flat on the cake beneath, its nose turned upwards in patient co-operation.

'I knew she wouldn't be able to get away from *something* polar,' Louisa said.

'Can I get my dress on now?' asked Rose. It was nearly one o'clock and the wedding was at two. Japhet, still in his dressing-gown, was drinking a glass of milk under the stairs, where he had gone again to look for a hammer and nails to put up that horseshoe. Their father was out seeing to the car; Louisa was collecting the latest batch of Christmas cards from the front-door mat.

'Don't open those now,' said her mother; but Louisa had spotted one which was not a card: it had a three-penny stamp, and was addressed to her. She went to the bathroom to read it in peace.

It was typed, on paper headed 'Rural District Council'. To her amazement it began: 'Dear Miss Brown,' and went on in such formal language that at first she hardly took it in.

When she did, she rushed downstairs, beaming.

'Look at this! They've written to thank me for what I did that night at the Fire Station! They're mad!' – beaming even more broadly. 'They say, "We would like to register our grateful appreciation of your valuable services" – and then about the time, and the day, and where it was – and listen, they actually end up, "Yours with every good wish for the coming year"!'

'Isn't that nice!' said Japhet, always readily touched by such things.

'It's signed just squiggle, then in brackets, "Clerk to the Council".'

'I need doing up,' said Rose, who had put on her white dress back to front. Louisa turned it round for her, and did her up, and tied the rose-pink ribbon sash; she didn't at all mind not being a bridesmaid now; the letter was ample compensation. She planned to frame it and put it up in her room between the signed photograph of a TV star (Georgia's gift) and the Dutch stick-on picture she had done in kindergarten.

At half-past one, Edith came down from her little room with the grated-apple dish in one hand and her bouquet of Christmas roses in the other.

'Gosh, you look quite different!' said Japhet, meaning it as a perfect compliment.

At twenty to two, their mother was looking for a safety-pin.

167

At a quarter to, Japhet was told to brush his hair, and said he had.

At ten to, Edith, Louisa, Rose and their mother were packed in the car, ready to drive to the church: it was about half a mile up the road. Japhet and his father were to walk, and had started already.

Rose, peering out of the window to make sure that Oats was not following, noticed how every stiff stalk of dead cow-parsley, bramble or chopped hedge was lined with frost. 'Isn't it beautiful!' she began, awe-struck. . . . Then the car broke down.

There was now barely half a mile to go – but you could hardly expect Edith to walk that, along the frost-tufted verge, in a long white dress and silver shoes. And Rose would probably fall over.

Louisa said, 'This would happen to us!' and bellowed despairingly up the road in the direction where her father and Japhet had gone; they were tiny figures rounding the bend in the white distance.

Had they heard? She thought she saw them hesitate; she bellowed again. Her mother plugged away at the self-starter. No response.

'It'll have to be Shanks's pony,' said Edith, and Rose was just going to ask what that meant when the miracle happened.

Or if not a miracle, at any rate something very extra-ordinary and lucky indeed.

Japhet had heard Louisa shout, the second time;

he and his father were standing in the middle of the road waving their arms about and shouting back when a lorry clattered round the bend and pulled up with a squeal, only just in time not to knock them over.

'Much too fast, on these frosty roads. . . .' their father began.

'You want to mind out,' said a voice.

Then Japhet saw a bald head and a huge moustache. And the words 'Pinks Ladders'.

'Hallo,' he said, 'it's you.'

'Hey,' said the man, 'you're one of them I cut the 'air of. What's 'appened to that, then? You've been and gone and grown it!'

'We're going to a wedding,' said Japhet, 'and our car seems to have broken down – along the road there.'

'The bride's in it,' said his father. 'And the brides-maid, and – oh, for heavens' sake, I'm sure it was all right this morning.' And he started to run back to-wards the old car, which stood alone and marooned in the frosty distance. Small female figures could now be seen scuttling round it.

' 'Old on,' said the man in the lorry, 'I'll give you a lift. What's the matter – hop in!'

Their father hesitated, looked at his watch and hopped. It was nearly two o'clock.

They found Edith and Rose anxiously starting to walk. Louisa, with a very red face, was trying to push the car from behind. Her mother sat at the wheel, distraught.

'What sort of a caper's this, then?' said the man with the moustache. 'They can't do that: they can't *walk* to church! 'Ooever 'eard of such a thing?'

And with a tremendous roar of the engine he turned his lorry almost full circle, lumping it backwards nearly into the ditch, up and out again.

'Come on,' he said, 'all of you. I can take the lot, I'm empty. Pack in. Bride and cetera in front, it's cleaner. The rest'll have to rattle about.'

They looked at each other.

'We're late as it is,' said Louisa.

'Perhaps I *should* have had a hired car. . . .' Edith began vaguely.

'What's the matter with this, then?' said the man. 'You've got something original 'ere. And not only that, but fast! Come on, how much longer are you going to keep the poor bloke waiting?'

So they all climbed in, and the man started up almost before their father had chained up the back flap.

'I bet they've never 'ad a party arrive like this,' the man said happily. 'I bet you're makin' 'istory, you lot. People are too cut-and-dried, that's what's the matter these days. . . .' But this train of thought was cut short as he nearly shot right past the church, and those in the back stood up and shouted, so that he brought the lorry to a violent standstill with another squeal of brakes.

Breathless and shaken, they clambered out.

'Thank you,' said their father, 'very kind.'

'Indeed,' said Edith. 'I'm afraid I can't offer you any-thing, but—'

'Look, stop gassin' and get on in,' said the man. 'There's a limit to what the fondest chap'll wait. And good luck!'

'Perhaps I ought to have asked him to come in him-self,' said Edith as she walked up the path. 'It seems a little ungrateful.'

'He was wearing blue overalls,' said Louisa, 'he wouldn't have felt right.'

The little church was warm and lit, and decorated all over with holly. There was a Christmas tree and a crib, twines of ivy round the pillars and great white lilies at the altar.

It was a lovely wedding, Louisa thought. She had never been to one before. Mr Browne looked very serious indeed, but happy. David just looked serious; Edith just happy. Rose didn't drop her prayer-book; their father gave Edith away with such dignity that you would never have known he had been rushed to church in Pinks's Ladders.

But Japhet's chief joy was the party afterwards. To begin with, another miracle: there was the man with the moustache waiting for them outside the church –

in a different car! No lorry – but a sleek black affair with room for them all to cram in, cushioned and luxuriously-sprung. It even added to the glamour, by contrast, that the man was still in his blue overalls.

'How did you do it?' Japhet kept asking on the way home.

'Ways and means,' said the man with a huge wink. 'Ways and means. Well, I thought to meself, 'ow are they going to get back, then? So I did a bit of nippin' around.'

And Japhet could get no more out of him than that: except the solemn assurance that if more people did a bit more nippin' around in this life, they wouldn't be so dug in. Japhet thought about this quite a lot afterwards. The man refused to come in to the party, and they have never seen him again from that day to this. But Japhet still sometimes wonders where he is nipping around now.

Georgia did come to the party, dropped by Jaguar; so did Podge, by bus. So did the wool-shop lady: Louisa had suggested asking her, and their mother had agreed, she was so grateful to have had that dress in time. Neither Edith nor Mr Browne had asked anybody, nor had Rose: being a bridesmaid was enough for her.

There had been one terrible moment on the way home when their mother had gasped, 'Oats! Where did we leave him?' – thinking of all that food spread about, and of the day when Oats had once eaten a whole laid tea, except for the jelly, which he had no doubt licked.

But he was safely shut in the play-room with what their father was beginning to call That Cat.

Nothing particular happened at the party, but the house seemed very full, and everyone ate a lot and drank whatever came, whether it was coffee or tea or champagne or Coke or Japhet's cold milk; and Louisa actually saw Mr Browne smile – not once, but on and on.

And Podge stood about looking sheepish until he had had so many mince-pies that he relaxed and did his card trick. And Georgia had brought her recorder, so they all sang carols and a mixture of other things such as *Auld Lang Syne, Home, Sweet Home*, and *There's a Hole in My Bucket* – Japhet's favourite.

Japhet and Rose rushed about handing round food, and Japhet kept saying, 'Isn't this nice!' looking very pink and surprised. They had never had such a party in this house before, and he couldn't think why. He was delighted to see so many people eating so much. This is life, he thought to himself, and wished he could tell the man with the moustache. Meanwhile, there was one slice of French bread left, but when he asked his mother if he could eat it, she said, 'Hand it round first.' So he took it from room to room in his hand, saying, 'Anybody want this?' They could see he hoped they wouldn't, so of course they didn't. In a glow of Christmas spirit he shared it with Podge, and was completely happy.

And the presents! These would have stuffed the house, even without the people. Wedding presents, Christmas presents, bridesmaid's presents, bride's present to groom, groom's to bride. . . . We couldn't possibly tell you them all. The floor was thick with wrapping-paper and dropped labels, and the wool-shop lady was seen anxiously winding up bits of ribbon and gold string. But she couldn't keep up with it all, and sang *Roses of Picardy* instead, in a surprising contralto.

Here are a few of the presents:

Rose, as bridesmaid, had a gold locket with an enamelled robin on it; it had belonged to Mr Browne's mother.

The bride gave the groom a waterproof watch.

The groom gave the bride a silver serviette ring with curled initials engraved: 'E.B.'

'I shall use it on Sundays,' said Edith.

She gave Louisa a book on wild flowers and Japhet one on animals.

'I do *hope* they didn't ill-treat them,' she said, 'to get those photographs.'

Japhet showed her the bison and she was reassured.

All three children joined together to give Edith a bird-bath. This, she whispered to Louisa, was quite her nicest present.

David had things too, of course, and so did everyone else – but there were far too many to mention now. Louisa decided to make a list. 'Otherwise we shall forget who's given who what.' Japhet didn't see that it mattered, as long as everyone had a good time. Louisa thought how different he was from her.

'I want to remember it all properly,' she said.

'I couldn't forget my robin,' said Rose, 'even if I tried. And I shan't try.'

'You'd better get a safety-catch put on it,' said Louisa. Somebody in the family had to be practical.

And if you are practical, too, you may ask: what next? A party must end, and Christmas be over, and New Year not only begin but go on, and on. . . .

They had another smaller party this New Year's Eve: just themselves and Edith and Mr Browne and David; with games round the fire, and crackers, and a peculiar hot drink as the TV struck midnight. The children were so pleased to be up till that time that they drank it without complaint; and no one else liked to say anything.

And then? Well, Louisa really summed it up to Georgia as they sat in the school cloakroom eating chocolate one spring afternoon.

'It's funny,' she said, 'how people change. Or perhaps they were really like it all the time. What do you think?'

'Search me,' said Georgia cheerfully, 'what people?'

'Edith,' said Louisa, 'and Mr Browne. Honestly. I'd never have believed it: there she is actually making cakes! Of course they have to be done with some special Health Flour and they're rather queer, but still . . . And she cleans, and mends, and helps David with his Latin. And they wash-up after every meal. And Mr Browne goes about smiling—'

'What, all the time?'

'I'm not there all the time; I go on Saturdays. Anyway, he never smiled at all before. Of course he still has his old bike and his Tilley lamp – he sticks to those – but otherwise, you'd think he was a changed man!'

'Perhaps he is,' said Georgia.

'I don't know.' Louisa was thoughtful. 'I wonder if people do change. Grown-ups. Or if it's just—'

'Just what?'

Louisa sighed. There were things you couldn't really explain to Georgia; perhaps not to anybody.

Things, for instance, such as her feeling of sadness when she had heard that old Mrs Birch had died on Boxing Day. Georgia never understood why Louisa minded so much that she had never been round to play draughts; and Louisa discovered that some shadows had to be kept to yourself.

But this was her only one: everything else promised fair.

'What about those mushrooms?' asked Georgia.

'Edith has decided to grow herbs,' said Louisa, 'and in the summer, sweet-peas.'

Japhet was already planning to make Edith a stand for the roadside, with a bucket and a 'Cut Flowers' notice chalked on the play-room blackboard.

'It sounds rather nice,' said Georgia.

Louisa thought so too; but she would never look at a sweet-pea, or a mushroom, or Edith, or the new Tilley lamp Mr Browne gave Japhet for his birthday – or a lot of other things – without wondering how much of all this would have happened without the night the rain came in.